BEAT *the* CLOCK
CHICKEN

In all Rodale cookbooks, our mission is to provide delicious and nutritious recipes. Our recipes also meet the standards of the Rodale Test Kitchen for dependability, ease, practicality, and, most of all, great taste. To give us your comments, call (800) 848-4735.

RODALE'S
New
Classics™

BEAT *the* CLOCK
CHICKEN

By Anne Egan

RODALE

Cover and Interior Designer: Richard Kershner

Cover and Interior Photos: Rodale Images

Front Cover Recipe: Lemon-Rosemary Chicken (page 43)

Library of Congress Cataloging-in-Publication Data

Egan, Anne.

   Beat the clock chicken / by Anne Egan.

       p.   cm. — (Rodale's new classics)

   Includes index.

   ISBN 1–57954–396–0 paperback

    1. Cookery (Chicken)   2. Quick and easy cookery.   I. Title.

  TX750.5.C45 E36   2001

  641.6'65—dc21   00–011164

Distributed to the book trade by St. Martin's Press

2 4 6 8 10 9 7 5 3 1 paperback

Visit us on the Web at www.rodalecookbooks.com, or call us toll-free at (800) 848-4735.

RODALE

WE **INSPIRE** AND **ENABLE** PEOPLE TO IMPROVE
THEIR LIVES AND THE WORLD AROUND THEM

**ZESTY
CHICKEN WITH
CORN SALSA**
Page 15

**ROAST
CHICKEN WITH
VEGETABLES**
Page 40

Contents

**CRISPY CAJUN
CHICKEN**
Page 76

**CHINESE
CHICKEN
SALAD**
Page 96

Introduction

Everyone loves chicken—and why not? It's versatile, inexpensive, low-fat, and delicious. Whether a whole roasted bird, cut into pieces on the bone, or—the most popular—boneless, skinless breasts, chicken makes dinner a breeze to prepare. Chicken works with just about every seasoning blend and potential sauce. A simple herb rub is just as tasty as a rich cream sauce.

To be sure you never tire of chicken, you'll want to vary the way you prepare it. And with today's busy lifestyles, no one has time to spend hours getting dinner on the table. *Rodale's New Classics* shows you the way. It's about enjoying the process of cooking while feeling confident that you are feeding your family the best foods possible. This is achieved by using the fastest ingredients and cooking techniques available.

Most of these chicken dishes use quick-cooking cuts like boneless, skinless breasts and thighs, as in

Zesty Chicken with Corn Salsa. When a whole chicken is featured, as in my Roast Chicken with Vegetables, the preparation time is minimal so that you can tend to other tasks or simply relax while it cooks.

Poultry Primer

Chicken is something that most everyone has cooked—we all have a few standard recipes that we prepare regularly. But there is more to chicken knowledge than meets the eye. Whether it is cooking with the latest cuts such as the boneless, skinless thighs, as in Honey-Mustard Chicken Dinner, or learning a new technique like butterflying a whole bird, as in Lemon-Rosemary Chicken, here are all the basics you will need to become a chicken expert.

Chicken Cuts. Today more than ever, chicken is available in every conceivable shape and size. Here is a list of the basic cuts and how they are best used.

▶ Whole chickens are available two ways. Young roasters are large, meaty birds that usually weigh 5 to 8 pounds and are perfect for roasting whole. The broiler-fryer is a bit smaller, weighing 3 to 4½ pounds. Broiler-fryers are great for roasting whole or butterflying. Cutting up a broiler-fryer is an inexpensive way to serve chicken parts.

Whole chickens are also available already cut up. This more convenient form is a bit more expensive than cutting up a whole bird yourself, but it saves on time and work.

▶ Chicken breasts, a favorite because they are lower in fat than the legs, are available boned and skinned or bone-in, either with the skin or skinned. Boneless, skinless breasts are the most commonly used cut, but don't ignore the bone-in version; they are great when baked bathed in sauce or lightly coated. When preparing boneless breasts or cutlets, look for thinly sliced boneless breasts. They're cut so thin, you won't need to pound them.

▶ Chicken legs are sold whole or cut into thighs and drumsticks. The legs are gaining in popularity, and with good reason. They are full-flavored and moist, and kids love them. Boneless, skinless thighs are now readily available and make a nice alternative to boneless, skinless breasts. Plan on two thighs or drumsticks per adult serving.

▶ Chicken wings are best known as an appetizer, slathered in a hot sauce. Use the first section, the drummettes, for these dishes because they are the part of the wing that carries all the meat. You will avoid having to cut off and discard the second section.

▶ Made from coarsely ground thigh meat, ground chicken makes great burgers, meatballs, or chili. Handle ground chicken very quickly as it tends to get mushy if overworked.

Purchasing. If your grocery shopping is one of many on a list of errands, always make it the last stop. Getting the groceries into the refrigerator as soon as possible helps prevent the food from overheating and possibly spoiling.

Although the meat and poultry aisles are often the first you'll come to in supermarkets, shop them last. This will keep your poultry cold longer. After you have made your selection, place the chicken in a plastic bag to prevent possible contamination to other groceries.

Storing. Be sure to get chicken in the refrigerator as soon as possible after purchasing. Store raw chicken in the coldest part of your refrigerator, usually in the back and often on the top shelf. You will want the temperature to be 40°F. You can test different shelves with a refrigerator thermometer to determine which are the coldest. The doors are usually a bit warmer than the interior, so avoid storing chicken there. Keep the chicken in the original package placed on a plate for up to 2 days.

Cooked chicken should be covered and refrigerated as soon as possible, but no longer than 2 hours after cooking. Chicken parts keep for up to 2 days in the refrigerator. A whole chicken will last up to 3 days. Freeze any cooked chicken that will not be used in these times.

Freezing. Raw whole chicken may be frozen for up to 1 year if wrapped in tightly sealed packing. Parts can be frozen for up to 9 months.

Always thaw raw chicken in the refrigerator. It is best to give it at least 24 hours to thaw completely. Leave the chicken in its wrapper and place on a plate to catch any dripping. For a quick thaw, place the chicken in its wrapper or a water-tight plastic bag and immerse it in a bowl of cold water on the countertop. Be sure to change the water frequently—about every 30 minutes. This method will have a whole chicken ready to cook in about 2 hours. Parts will be ready sooner.

Cooked chicken should be placed in a tightly sealed container or freezer food storage bag and used within 4 months. Thaw the cooked chicken in the refrigerator in its wrapping. Giving the chicken 24 hours to thaw is best.

Preparing. Rinse the chicken after removing it from the packaging. Place on paper towels to drain and then pat dry. Or, place the rinsed chicken in a colander in the sink to dry.

After preparation, be sure to wash all counters, cutting boards, knives, and other utensils with soapy water before working with any other foods. Also, be sure to wash your hands before moving on to further food prep.

Cooking. For the moistest meat, cook the chicken with the skin on whenever possible. This will trap in moisture. Don't worry about extra calories since none of the fat of the skin will seep into the meat. Remove the skin before eating to save approximately 50 calories and 6 grams of fat per serving.

Chicken must be completely cooked to prevent food-borne illnesses. Taking a temperature is the best way to ensure that the bird is properly cooked. An instant-read thermometer is best for this job. Available at most supermarkets and cookware shops, these small items are well worth the price—you will use them not only for most chicken dishes but for meat as well. The internal temperature should reach 180°F for a whole chicken, 170°F for bone-in parts, and 160°F for boneless parts. At these temperatures, the juices will be clear, not pink, when the chicken is pierced.

Place marinating chicken in the refrigerator. One of the simplest ways I have found to marinate is to use a zip-top plastic food storage bag. Combine the marinade ingredients in the bag and then add the chicken.

Seal the bag and turn to coat well. The marinade is often discarded, but if a recipe calls for its use, be sure to bring the marinade to a full boil and boil for at least 3 minutes. Do not brush uncooked marinade onto cooked chicken.

Place cooked chicken on a clean plate—not the unwashed one that held the raw chicken. This happens most when grilling, so be sure to wash the plate while the chicken sizzles.

Whether you are preparing a special candlelight dinner for two or a simple weeknight meal, chicken will always fit the bill. All of these dishes are packed with flavor, easy to prepare, and sure to become family favorites. So spread your wings and have fun preparing chicken in a whole new way. Enjoy!

Anne Egan

IN THE
SKILLET

Chicken Parmesan

8 ounces fettuccine

3 tablespoons seasoned dried bread crumbs

3 tablespoons grated Parmesan cheese

1 tablespoon minced garlic

½ teaspoon freshly ground black pepper

4 boneless, skinless chicken breast halves

1 tablespoon olive oil

2 cups prepared marinara sauce

This classic Italian dish is a breeze to make with the help of prepared marinara sauce. For a change of pace, cut the chicken into thick strips or "fingers." The kids will love it.

Prepare fettuccine according to package directions.

Meanwhile, in a shallow bowl, combine the bread crumbs, cheese, garlic, and pepper. Add the chicken breasts, one at a time, and press into the mixture to coat both sides.

Heat the oil in a large skillet over medium-high heat. Add the chicken and cook, turning occasionally, for 12 minutes, or until a thermometer inserted in the thickest portion registers 160°F and the juices run clear. Remove to a plate and keep warm.

Add the marinara sauce to the skillet and cook over medium heat for 4 minutes, or until heated through.

Place the fettuccine on a serving plate and top with the chicken and marinara sauce.

Makes 4 servings

Per serving: 475 calories, 44 g protein, 43 g carbohydrates, 13 g fat, 143 mg cholesterol, 4 g fiber, 696 mg sodium

Zesty Chicken with Corn Salsa

2   teaspoons chili powder
2   teaspoons brown sugar
1   teaspoon ground cumin
4   boneless, skinless chicken breast halves
2   tablespoons olive oil
1   can (8 ounces) corn, drained
½   small red pepper, chopped
½   small cucumber, seeded and chopped
½   cup red kidney beans, rinsed and drained
3   tablespoons lime juice
¼   teaspoon salt

Chili powder and ground cumin add zing to chicken breasts. Served atop a flavorful salsa, this dish is delicious every day, yet pleasing enough for company.

In a cup, combine the chili powder, brown sugar, and cumin. Rub both sides of the chicken breasts with the spice mixture.

Heat the oil in a large skillet over medium heat. Add the chicken and cook, turning occasionally, for 12 minutes, or until a thermometer inserted in the thickest portion registers 160°F and the juices run clear.

Meanwhile, in a medium bowl, combine the corn, red pepper, cucumber, kidney beans, lime juice, and salt.

Evenly divide the corn salsa onto 4 plates. Top each with a chicken breast.

Makes 4 servings

Per serving: 287 calories, 30 g protein, 21 g carbohydrates, 9 g fat, 66 mg cholesterol, 5 g fiber, 461 mg sodium

COOKING TIP

Chili powder is a blend of dried herbs and spices. Typically, it is a mixture of dried chile peppers, garlic, cumin, coriander, cloves, and oregano. The color of chili powder can vary from light red to a dark red that is almost brown. These differences cause color changes in your dish, but the great flavor will be the same.

Herbed Chicken on Fettuccine

8   **ounces spinach fettuccine**

¼   **cup unbleached all-purpose flour**

½   **teaspoon salt**

½   **teaspoon freshly ground black pepper**

4   **boneless, skinless chicken breast halves**

2   **tablespoons olive oil**

2   **cloves garlic, minced**

½   **cup chicken broth**

3   **tablespoons lemon juice**

2   **tablespoons chopped fresh basil and/or oregano**

This simple yet flavorful dish comes together in just minutes. Add a tossed salad and you'll have a hearty, family-pleasing meal with little effort.

Prepare the fettuccine according to package directions.

On a plate, combine the flour, salt, and pepper. Add the chicken, one breast at a time, pressing to coat with the flour mixture.

Heat the oil in a large skillet over medium heat. Add the chicken and cook, turning occasionally, for 8 minutes. Push chicken to sides of the skillet. Add the garlic and cook, stirring frequently, for 1 minute. Add the chicken broth, lemon juice, and basil and/or oregano. Bring to a boil over high heat. Reduce the heat to low, cover, and simmer for 4 minutes, or until a thermometer inserted in the thickest portion of a breast registers 160°F and the juices run clear.

Evenly divide the fettuccine onto 4 plates. Top each with a chicken breast and drizzle with the broth mixture.

Makes 4 servings
Per serving: 330 calories, 34 g protein, 38 g carbohydrates, 4 g fat, 124 mg cholesterol, 2 g fiber, 457 mg sodium

Basil Marinara Chicken and Pasta

8   **ounces fusilli or spaghetti**

2   **tablespoons olive oil**

1   **medium onion, cut into wedges**

¼   **teaspoon salt**

¼   **teaspoon freshly ground black pepper**

2   **cloves garlic, minced**

4   **boneless, skinless chicken breast halves**

3   **cups prepared marinara sauce**

¼   **cup packed fresh basil leaves, cut into thin strips**

This child-friendly meal will please the kid in everyone. Prepared marinara sauce makes it simple enough for a last-minute supper.

Prepare the fusilli or spaghetti according to package directions.

Meanwhile, heat 1 tablespoon of the oil in a large skillet over medium-high heat. Add the onion, salt, and pepper and cook, stirring occasionally, for 4 minutes. Add the garlic and cook, stirring occasionally, for 2 minutes. Remove to a plate and keep warm.

Heat the remaining 1 tablespoon oil in the same skillet over medium heat. Add the chicken and cook, turning occasionally, for 4 minutes. Return the onion mixture to the skillet. Stir in the marinara sauce. Bring to a boil over high heat. Reduce the heat to low, cover, and simmer for 10 minutes, or until a thermometer inserted in the thickest portion registers 160°F and the juices run clear. Stir in the basil.

Place the fusilli or spaghetti on a serving platter. Top with the chicken and sauce.

Makes 4 servings

Per serving: 528 calories, 37 g protein, 57 g carbohydrates, 15 g fat, 66 mg cholesterol, 5 g fiber, 935 mg sodium

One-Dish Dinner

1½ pounds boneless, skinless chicken breasts, cut into strips
½ teaspoon dried thyme
¼ teaspoon salt
¼ teaspoon freshly ground black pepper
2 tablespoons olive oil
1 large onion, chopped
1 package (8 ounces) sliced mushrooms
1¾ cups chicken broth
1 box (6–7 ounces) rice pilaf mix

Mushrooms, onion, and chicken are scented with thyme and tossed with rice pilaf in this simple yet hearty dish.

Sprinkle the chicken with thyme, salt, and pepper.

Heat 1 tablespoon of the oil in a large skillet over medium-high heat. Add the chicken and cook, stirring occasionally, for 6 minutes, or until browned and no longer pink. Remove to a plate and keep warm.

Heat remaining 1 tablespoon of oil in the same skillet over medium heat. Add the onion and mushrooms and cook, stirring occasionally, for 8 minutes, or until very soft. Remove to the plate with the chicken.

Add the broth to the skillet. Bring to a boil over high heat. Add the rice mix and cook according to package directions. When rice is cooked, stir in the chicken and vegetables and heat through.

Makes 6 servings
Per serving: 278 calories, 31 g protein, 24 g carbohydrates, 7 g fat, 66 mg cholesterol, 2 g fiber, 750 mg sodium

Florida Chicken

¼   **cup + 1 tablespoon olive or vegetable oil**

1   **can (8 ounces) pineapple chunks in juice, drained and 3 tablespoons juice reserved**

2   **tablespoons orange juice**

2   **tablespoons brown sugar**

1   **tablespoon chopped mint**

½   **teaspoon ground ginger**

1   **orange, cut into sections**

½   **cup sliced strawberries**

4   **boneless, skinless chicken breast halves**

8   **ounces spinach leaves**

The flavors of sunny days are present in this lovely warm salad. Sweet fruit makes a delicate sauce for chicken and spinach.

In a medium bowl, whisk together ¼ cup oil, 3 tablespoons reserved pineapple juice, orange juice, brown sugar, mint, and ginger.

Remove 3 tablespoons of the marinade to another medium bowl and add the pineapple, orange, and strawberries. Toss to coat.

Add the chicken to the remaining marinade, tossing to coat. Cover and marinate for 15 minutes in the refrigerator.

Remove the chicken from the marinade, reserving the marinade.

Heat the remaining 1 tablespoon oil in a large skillet over medium-high heat. Add the chicken and cook, turning occasionally, for 12 minutes, or until a thermometer inserted in the thickest portion registers 160°F and the juices run clear.

Line 4 plates with the spinach. Top each with a chicken breast.

Add the reserved marinade to the skillet and bring to a boil over high heat. Boil for 3 minutes, stirring to remove brown bits from the pan. Evenly divide the hot marinade and fruit mixture over the chicken and spinach.

Makes 4 servings

Per serving: 381 calories, 35 g protein, 18 g carbohydrates, 19 g fat, 82 mg cholesterol, 7 g fiber, 162 mg sodium

Chicken Lo Mein

- 8 ounces lo mein noodles or thin spaghetti
- 2 tablespoons sesame or olive oil
- 1 pound boneless, skinless chicken breasts, cut into thin strips
- 1 onion, chopped
- 1 large red bell pepper, chopped
- 2 large cloves garlic, minced
- 1 cup snow peas
- ½ cup chicken broth
- 3 tablespoons rice wine vinegar
- 3 tablespoons soy sauce
- 1 tablespoon freshly grated ginger

The flavors of Asia are abundant in this colorful dish. Serve with a spinach and mandarin orange salad with ginger vinaigrette to complete the meal. For fun, finish with fortune cookies.

Prepare noodles according to package directions.

Meanwhile, heat 1 tablespoon of the oil in a large skillet over medium-high heat. Add the chicken and cook, stirring occasionally, for 6 minutes, or until browned and no longer pink. Remove to a plate and keep warm.

Heat the remaining 1 tablespoon oil in the same skillet over medium-high heat. Add the onion, pepper, garlic, and snow peas and cook, stirring occasionally, for 8 minutes, or until tender-crisp. Stir in the chicken broth, vinegar, soy sauce, and ginger and cook for 2 minutes. Add the chicken and noodles and heat through.

Makes 4 servings
Per serving: 436 calories, 35 g protein, 50 g carbohydrates, 9 g fat, 66 mg cholesterol, 3 g fiber, 923 mg sodium

Chicken with Creamy Mustard Sauce

3   tablespoons butter
1   pound thin-sliced boneless, skinless chicken breasts
2   large shallots, sliced
½   teaspoon dried thyme
1   tablespoon flour
¾   cup chicken broth
1   tablespoon coarse Dijon mustard
¼   cup half-and-half or heavy cream

This simple dish is elegant enough for your fussiest guest. Chicken cutlets bathed in a thyme-mustard cream sauce make an impressive main dish that comes together in less than 15 minutes. Serve with rice pilaf and steamed snap peas for a lovely presentation.

Melt 2 tablespoons of the butter in a large skillet over medium-high heat. Add the chicken and cook, turning occasionally, for 5 minutes, or until browned and no longer pink. Remove to serving platter and keep warm.

Melt the remaining 1 tablespoon of butter in the same skillet over medium-high heat. Add shallots and thyme and cook, stirring occasionally, for 4 minutes, or until soft. Sprinkle the flour over the shallots and cook, stirring constantly, for 1 minute. Stir in the broth and mustard. Bring to a boil and continue boiling, stirring frequently, for 1 minute, or until slightly thickened. Stir in the cream and heat through.

Place the sauce over the chicken.

Makes 4 servings
Per serving: 241 calories, 27 g protein, 4 g carbohydrates, 13 g fat, 97 mg cholesterol, 1 g fiber, 302 mg sodium

Sweet-and-Sour Chicken

1   cup white rice

2   tablespoons olive or vegetable oil

1   pound boneless, skinless chicken breasts, cut into 1" pieces

1   medium onion, thinly sliced

1   small red bell pepper, cut into thin strips

1   package (8 ounces) sliced mushrooms

1   teaspoon five-spice powder

1   can (8 ounces) pineapple chunks in juice, drained with ¼ cup juice reserved

1   jar (10 ounces) sweet-and-sour sauce

2   tablespoons rice wine vinegar

Who needs takeout when this delicious meal can be prepared faster than delivery? The five-spice powder adds a subtle flavor to the prepared sweet-and-sour sauce, which brings the ingredients together well.

Prepare the rice according to package directions.

Meanwhile, heat 1 tablespoon of the oil in a large skillet over medium-high heat. Add the chicken and cook, stirring occasionally, for 6 minutes, or until browned and no longer pink. Remove to a plate and keep warm.

Add the remaining 1 tablespoon oil to the same skillet. Add the onion, pepper, mushrooms, and five-spice powder and cook, stirring occasionally, for 8 minutes, or until tender-crisp.

Return the chicken to the skillet. Stir in the pineapple with reserved juice, sweet-and-sour sauce, and vinegar. Heat through.

Evenly divide the rice among 4 bowls and top with the chicken mixture.

Makes 4 servings
Per serving: 491 calories, 32 g protein, 68 g carbohydrates, 10 g fat, 66 mg cholesterol, 3 g fiber, 311 mg sodium

Chicken Paprikash

8 ounces egg noodles

1 pound boneless, skinless chicken breast halves, cut into strips

½ teaspoon salt

¼ teaspoon freshly ground black pepper

2 tablespoons olive oil

1 large onion, chopped

1 red bell pepper, cut into strips

1 tablespoon paprika

1 can (14½ ounces) diced tomatoes

½ cup (4 ounces) sour cream

A creamy tomato sauce coats chicken and vegetables in this traditional Hungarian dish. For a healthier change of pace, serve over spinach noodles.

Prepare the egg noodles according to package directions.

Meanwhile, season the chicken with the salt and black pepper. Heat 1 tablespoon of the oil in a large skillet over medium-high heat. Add the chicken and cook, stirring occasionally, for 5 minutes, or until just browned. Remove to a plate and keep warm.

Heat the remaining 1 tablespoon oil in the same skillet over medium-high heat. Add the onion, bell pepper, and paprika and cook, stirring occasionally, for 5 minutes. Stir in the tomatoes and chicken. Bring to a boil. Reduce the heat to low, cover, and simmer for 5 minutes, or until chicken is no longer pink. Remove the skillet from the heat and stir in sour cream.

Place the noodles in a serving bowl and top with the chicken mixture.

Makes 4 servings
Per serving: 548 calories, 39 g protein, 63 g carbohydrates, 16 g fat, 130 mg cholesterol, 8 g fiber, 800 mg sodium

Chicken with Black Beans and Rice

1   **cup converted white rice**

2   **tablespoons olive oil**

1   **pound boneless, skinless chicken thighs, cut into strips**

3   **scallions, cut into 1" pieces**

1   **red bell pepper, chopped**

¼   **teaspoon chili powder**

½   **teaspoon dried oregano**

1   **cup chicken broth**

1   **can (15 ounces) black beans, rinsed and drained**

1   **can (14½ ounces) whole peeled tomatoes**

1   **can (4 ounces) chopped green chilies**

Don't be alarmed by the long ingredient list—this family-friendly skillet dinner actually comes together quite quickly. If you take a second glance, you'll notice that most of the ingredients are in your cupboard.

Prepare rice according to package directions.

Meanwhile, heat 1 tablespoon of the oil in a large skillet over medium-high heat. Add the chicken and cook, stirring occasionally, for 5 minutes, or until browned. Remove to a plate and keep warm.

Heat the remaining 1 tablespoon of oil in the same skillet over medium-high heat. Add the scallions, pepper, chili powder, and oregano and cook, stirring occasionally, for 5 minutes, or until the vegetables are tender-crisp.

Stir in the broth, beans, tomatoes (with juice), chilies, and chicken, using a spoon to break up the tomatoes. Bring to a boil. Reduce the heat to low, cover, and simmer for 5 minutes to blend the flavors. Stir in the rice.

Makes 4 servings

Per serving: 465 calories, 31 g protein, 60 g carbohydrates, 12 g fat, 94 mg cholesterol, 8 g fiber, 764 mg sodium

Tomato-Orange Chicken

1	package (6 ounces) rice pilaf mix
2	teaspoons brown sugar
2	teaspoons grated orange peel
¼	teaspoon freshly ground black pepper
4	boneless, skinless chicken breast halves
3	tablespoons olive oil
1	red onion, minced
4	ounces sliced mushrooms
1	can (14 ounces) diced tomatoes
⅓	cup orange juice
1	tablespoon chopped fresh thyme

Tomatoes and orange blend to form a fresh, flavorful sauce scented with thyme. Serve over rice pilaf for a hearty meal.

Prepare the rice pilaf according to package direction.

Meanwhile, in a cup, combine the brown sugar, orange peel, and pepper. Rub both sides of the chicken breasts with the mixture.

Heat 2 tablespoons of the oil in a large skillet over medium heat. Add the chicken and cook, turning occasionally, for 12 minutes, or until a thermometer inserted in the thickest portion registers 160°F and the juices run clear. Remove to a plate and keep warm.

Heat the remaining tablespoon of oil in the same skillet over medium-high heat. Add the onion and mushrooms and cook for 6 minutes, or until tender. Add the tomatoes (with juice), orange juice, and thyme, and bring to a boil over high heat. Reduce the heat to medium-low and simmer, uncovered, for 5 minutes, or until thickened

Evenly divide the pilaf onto 4 plates. Top each serving with a chicken breast and the tomato sauce.

Makes 4 servings
Per serving: 426 calories, 39 g protein, 39 g carbohydrates, 13 g fat, 82 mg cholesterol, 2 g fiber, 1,052 mg sodium

Chicken with Cranberry-Orange Sauce

1 **pound boneless, skinless chicken thighs**
½ **teaspoon salt**
¼ **teaspoon cracked black pepper**
2 **tablespoons olive oil**
⅓ **cup chicken broth**
1½ **cups (6 ounces) fresh or frozen cranberries**
¼ **cup orange juice**
⅓ **cup packed brown sugar**
⅛ **teaspoon ground cinnamon**

A sweet-tart sauce bathes tender chicken thighs. For a special presentation, use boneless, skinless breasts in place of the thighs.

Season the chicken with the salt and pepper. Heat the oil in a large skillet over medium-high heat. Add the chicken and cook, turning occasionally, for 6 minutes, or until browned. Add the broth and bring to a boil over high heat. Reduce the heat to low, cover, and simmer for 8 minutes, or until a thermometer inserted in the thickest portion of chicken registers 160°F and the juices run clear.

Meanwhile, in a medium saucepan, combine the cranberries, orange juice, brown sugar, and cinnamon. Bring to a boil over high heat. Reduce the heat to medium-low and simmer, stirring frequently, for 4 minutes, or until the cranberries pop.

Remove the chicken from the skillet and place on a serving platter. Return the skillet to the heat and increase the heat to high. Add the cranberry mixture to the skillet and cook for 2 minutes, stirring constantly. Pour the sauce over the chicken.

Makes 4 servings
Per serving: 268 calories, 23 g protein, 19 g carbohydrates, 11 g fat, 94 mg cholesterol, 2 g fiber, 441 mg sodium

Chicken Curry in a Hurry

2 tablespoons olive or vegetable oil

1 pound boneless, skinless chicken breast halves, cut into 1" pieces

1 onion, cut into wedges

1 red bell pepper, chopped

1½ teaspoons curry powder

¼ teaspoon ground allspice

1 can (14½ ounces) diced tomatoes

¼ cup raisins

If curry is new to your cooking repertoire, this dish is for you. Tomatoes, onion, and pepper blend with sweet raisins and pungent curry for a mild, yet flavorful dish. Serve over couscous or rice.

Heat 1 tablespoon of the oil in a large skillet over medium-high heat. Add the chicken and cook, stirring occasionally, for 5 minutes, or until browned. Remove to a plate and keep warm.

Heat the remaining 1 tablespoon of oil in the same skillet over medium-high heat. Add the onion, pepper, curry powder, and allspice and cook, stirring occasionally, for 5 minutes, or until the vegetables are tender.

Stir in the tomatoes (with juice), raisins, and chicken. Bring to a boil. Reduce the heat to low, cover, and simmer for 5 minutes, or until chicken is no longer pink.

Makes 4 servings

Per serving: 249 calories, 28 g protein, 15 g carbohydrates, 9 g fat, 66 mg cholesterol, 2 g fiber, 482 mg sodium

Szechuan Stir-Fry

1 cup converted white rice

5 tablespoons prepared stir-fry sauce

1 pound boneless, skinless chicken breasts, cut into 1" pieces

1 tablespoon freshly grated ginger

⅛ teaspoon ground red pepper

2 tablespoons vegetable oil

1 package (8 ounces) sliced mushrooms

4 ounces snow peas

1 medium red and/or yellow bell pepper, cut into strips

¾ cup chicken broth

1½ teaspoons cornstarch

Prepared stir-fry sauce makes this meal super-fast. The ground red pepper adds fire to the sauce—if you prefer a more mild dish, you can eliminate it.

Prepare the rice according to the package directions, adding 1 tablespoon of the stir-fry sauce to the water.

Meanwhile, in a medium bowl, combine the chicken, ginger, ground red pepper, and the remaining 4 tablespoons stir-fry sauce. Toss to coat.

Heat 1 tablespoon of the oil in a large skillet over medium-high heat. Add the chicken and cook, stirring occasionally, for 6 minutes, or until no longer pink. Remove to a plate and keep warm.

Heat the remaining 1 tablespoon oil in the same skillet over medium-high heat. Add the mushrooms, snow peas, and bell pepper and cook, stirring occasionally, for 8 minutes, or until tender-crisp.

In a small bowl, whisk together the broth and cornstarch until dissolved. Add to the skillet and bring to a boil over high heat. Return the chicken to the skillet. Continue cooking, stirring occasionally, for 2 minutes, or until the sauce thickens and the chicken is heated through.

Evenly divide the rice among 4 plates and top each with the chicken.

Makes 4 servings
Per serving: 414 calories, 33 g protein, 48 g carbohydrates, 10 g fat, 66 mg cholesterol, 3 g fiber, 851 mg sodium

Chicken Mozzarella

1 pound thin-sliced boneless, skinless chicken breasts

1 teaspoon dried Italian seasoning

2 tablespoons olive oil

1 medium red onion, chopped

1 green bell pepper, chopped

1 clove garlic, minced

2 cups chicken broth

1 cup (4 ounces) ditalini pasta or other small macaroni

1 medium tomato, seeded and chopped

1 cup (4 ounces) shredded mozzarella cheese

Simple comfort food is what you will find in this dish. Chicken, onion, pepper, and pasta float in a tomato broth that is splendid finished off with mozzarella cheese.

Season the chicken with the Italian seasoning. Heat 1 tablespoon of the oil in a large skillet over medium-high heat. Add the chicken and cook, stirring occasionally, for 5 minutes, or until browned. Remove to a plate and keep warm.

Heat the remaining 1 tablespoon of oil in the same skillet over medium-high heat. Add the onion, pepper, and garlic and cook, stirring occasionally, for 2 minutes. Add the broth. Bring to a boil over high heat. Stir in the pasta and cook over medium heat, stirring occasionally, for 8 minutes. Add the tomato and chicken to the skillet. Reduce the heat to low, cover, and simmer for 5 minutes, or until the chicken is no longer pink and the pasta is tender.

Remove from heat and sprinkle with the cheese. Cover and let stand for 2 minutes, or until the cheese is melted.

Makes 4 servings
Per serving: 394 calories, 36 g protein, 28 g carbohydrates, 15 g fat, 88 mg cholesterol, 2 g fiber, 470 mg sodium

Wild Chicken Marsala

1	pound thin-sliced boneless, skinless chicken breasts
¼	teaspoon salt
¼	teaspoon freshly ground black pepper
3	tablespoons olive oil
8	ounces assorted sliced mushrooms such as shiitake, portobello, and/or crimini
2	large cloves garlic, minced
¼	cup marsala wine
½	cup chicken broth
1	tablespoon flour

Wild mushrooms add an earthy flavor to this classic marsala sauce. Elegant enough for company, serve this dish with rice pilaf or buttered herbed noodles.

Season the chicken with the salt and pepper. Heat 2 tablespoons of the oil in a large skillet over medium-high heat. Add the chicken, in batches if necessary, and cook for 4 minutes, turning once. Remove to a plate and keep warm.

Heat the remaining 1 tablespoon of oil and cook the mushrooms and garlic, stirring occasionally, for 6 minutes, or until tender. Add the wine and cook for 2 minutes.

In a small bowl, whisk together the broth and flour until blended. Stir into the skillet. Bring to a boil over high heat. Return chicken to skillet. Reduce the heat to low and simmer for 2 minutes, or until the chicken is no longer pink and the sauce has thickened slightly.

Makes 4 servings
Per serving: 253 calories, 29 g protein, 4 g carbohydrates, 12 g fat, 66 mg cholesterol, 2 g fiber, 306 mg sodium

Updated Blue-Plate Special

1   **pound thin-sliced boneless, skinless chicken breasts**

½   **teaspoon salt**

¼   **teaspoon coarsely ground black pepper**

2   **tablespoons olive oil**

1   **package (8 ounces) mushrooms, sliced**

2   **tablespoons unbleached all-purpose flour**

1½ **cups chicken broth**

2   **tablespoons balsamic vinegar**

4   **thick slices focaccia or crusty Italian bread, toasted**

1   **tablespoon snipped fresh chives or thinly sliced scallion greens**

This contemporary version of the diner favorite takes an open-faced sandwich to new heights.

Season the chicken with the salt and pepper.

Heat 1 tablespoon of the oil in a large skillet over medium-high heat. Add the chicken, in batches if necessary, and cook, turning occasionally, for 4 minutes, or until golden brown and no longer pink. Remove to a plate and keep warm.

Heat the remaining 1 tablespoon of oil in the same skillet over medium heat. Add the mushrooms and cook, stirring occasionally, for 6 minutes, or until tender. Sprinkle the flour over the mushrooms and cook, stirring constantly, for 1 minute. Add the broth and vinegar and bring to a boil over high heat. Boil for 2 minutes.

Place one slice of bread on each of 4 plates. Evenly divide the chicken and mushroom sauce over each. Sprinkle with chives or scallions.

Makes 4 servings

Per serving: 308 calories, 31 g protein, 22 g carbohydrates, 10 g fat, 66 mg cholesterol, 1 g fiber, 757 mg sodium

Rigatoni with Herbed Chicken

8   ounces rigatoni pasta

1   pound boneless, skinless chicken breasts, cut into ½" chunks

1   clove garlic, minced

½   teaspoon fennel seeds, crushed

1   tablespoon olive or vegetable oil

1   can (14½ ounces) diced tomatoes

½   cup reduced-fat ricotta cheese

2   tablespoons chopped fresh basil or parsley

Fennel seeds and basil add a sweet flavor to this tomato cream sauce. Tossed with tender chicken and thick rigatoni, it is sure to become a family favorite.

Prepare the pasta according to package directions.

Meanwhile, in a medium bowl, combine the chicken, garlic, and fennel seeds. Toss until evenly coated.

Heat the oil in a large skillet over medium-high heat. Add the chicken mixture and cook, stirring occasionally, for 6 minutes, or until browned and almost done. Stir in the tomatoes (with juice) and cook, stirring occasionally, for 3 minutes, or until the chicken is no longer pink.

Place the rigatoni in a serving bowl. Top with the chicken mixture. Place the ricotta and basil over the sauce. Toss to serve.

Makes 4 servings

Per serving: 426 calories, 38 g protein, 47 g carbohydrates, 8 g fat, 75 mg cholesterol, 2 g fiber, 528 mg sodium

Thai Curried Chicken and Vegetables

8	ounces rice noodles or thin spaghetti
4	cups small broccoli florets
2	tablespoons olive or vegetable oil
1	pound boneless, skinless chicken thighs, cut into strips
3	cloves garlic, chopped
1	large onion, cut into wedges
1	red bell pepper, cut into 1" pieces
1	tablespoon minced fresh ginger
1	can (14 ounces) light coconut milk
⅓	cup chicken broth
1	tablespoon green curry paste
2	tablespoons Thai fish sauce or reduced-sodium soy sauce

The mild flavor of coconut milk contrasted with the zip of green curry paste makes a lively sauce—delicious tossed with rice noodles and vegetables.

Prepare the noodles according to package directions, adding the broccoli during the last 3 minutes of cooking. Drain and place in a large bowl.

Meanwhile, heat 1 tablespoon of the oil in a large skillet over medium-high heat. Add the chicken and cook, stirring, for 8 minutes, or until browned. Remove to a plate and keep warm.

Heat the remaining 1 tablespoon oil in the same skillet over medium-high heat. Add the garlic, onion, pepper, and ginger and cook, stirring occasionally, for 3 minutes. Add the coconut milk, broth, curry paste, fish sauce, and chicken. Bring to a boil over high heat. Reduce the heat to low and simmer, stirring occasionally, for 4 minutes, or until the chicken is no longer pink and the vegetables are tender-crisp.

Pour the sauce over the noodles and broccoli. Toss to coat. Top with the chicken mixture.

Makes 4 servings
Per serving: 411 calories, 28 g protein, 33 g carbohydrates, 19 g fat, 95 mg cholesterol, 4 g fiber, 839 mg sodium

COOKING TIP

The array of Thai ingredients in supermarkets is sure to add zest to many dishes. Try different curry pastes, sauces, and noodles. Be sure to use Thai light coconut milk and not cream of coconut, which is too thick and sweet for savory dishes.

FROM THE
OVEN

Roast Chicken with Vegetables

3   cloves garlic, minced
½   teaspoon salt
½   teaspoon freshly ground black pepper
1   chicken (about 3½ pounds)
1   pound small red potatoes, quartered
2   carrots, cut diagonally into 1½" pieces
1   onion, cut into wedges
¼   cup olive oil
3   tablespoons orange juice concentrate
3   tablespoons red wine vinegar
2   teaspoons fennel seeds, crushed
½   cup frozen peas, thawed

Roasting vegetables with a whole chicken gives them a lovely caramelized glaze. Be sure to serve the pan juices with this dish— they're brimming with rich flavors.

Preheat the oven to 375°F.

In a small bowl, combine the garlic, salt, and pepper.

Rinse the chicken and pat dry with paper towels. Remove and discard any excess fat from inside the chicken. Place the chicken, breast side up, on a rack in a shallow roasting pan. Using your fingers, gently loosen the skin from the breast meat and spread the garlic mixture under the skin.

In a large bowl, combine the potatoes, carrots, onion, oil, orange juice concentrate, vinegar, and fennel seeds. Arrange the vegetable mixture around the chicken in the pan. Roast the chicken, basting occasionally, for 40 minutes. Cover with foil and roast, basting occasionally, for 30 minutes longer. Add the peas to the pan and roast for an additional 10 minutes, or until a thermometer inserted in a breast registers 180°F and the juices run clear.

Remove the chicken to a serving platter. Using a slotted spoon, remove the vegetables to the platter with the chicken. Let stand for 10 minutes. Skim the fat from the pan drippings and discard the fat. Serve the pan juices alongside the chicken and vegetables.

Makes 6 servings
Per serving: 466 calories, 27 g protein, 19 g carbohydrates, 31 g fat, 96 mg cholesterol, 3 g fiber, 276 mg sodium

Lemon-Rosemary Chicken

1 chicken (about 3 pounds), butterflied (see tip)
3 large lemons
6 cloves garlic, quartered lengthwise
4 sprigs fresh rosemary
¼ cup chicken broth
3 tablespoons brown sugar
2 tablespoons olive or vegetable oil
1 tablespoon Dijon mustard

Packed with flavor and yet so moist, this roasted chicken makes an impressive presentation.

Preheat the oven to 375°F. Arrange the chicken, skin side up, in a 13" x 9" baking pan.

Slice 2 of the lemons. Using your fingers, gently loosen the skin from the breast meat and tuck half of the lemon slices, half of the garlic, and half of the rosemary sprigs under the skin along the breast meat. Lay the remaining lemon slices on top of the chicken.

Cut the remaining lemon in half and squeeze the juice into a small bowl. Add the remaining garlic, broth, brown sugar, oil, and mustard. Evenly pour the mixture over the chicken.

Roast, basting occasionally, for 1 hour, or until a thermometer inserted in a breast registers 180°F and the juices run clear. Let stand for 10 minutes before carving.

Garnish with the remaining 2 rosemary sprigs.

Makes 4 servings

Per serving: 314 calories, 41 g protein, 21 g carbohydrates, 9 g fat, 99 mg cholesterol, 4 g fiber, 175 mg sodium

COOKING TIP

You may have your butcher butterfly the chicken or do it yourself. To butterfly, cut through the ribs on either side of the backbone with a sharp knife or a pair of kitchen shears. Remove the bone and then turn the bird skin-side down. Press the palm of your hand hard against the breastbone to flatten the bird.

Crumbly Baked Chicken

¼ cup flour

1 tablespoon crab-boil seasoning

½ teaspoon salt

2 eggs

¾ cup cornflake crumbs

3 tablespoons grated Parmesan cheese

1 broiler-fryer chicken (2½–3 pounds), cut into serving pieces and skin removed

Similar to fried, these chicken parts are coated with a zesty, flavorful crust. The good news is that they are just as delicious as fried, but with a fraction of the fat.

Preheat the oven to 400°F. Coat a baking pan with cooking spray.

In a shallow bowl, combine the flour, crab-boil seasoning, and salt. In another bowl, beat the eggs. In a third shallow bowl, combine the cornflake crumbs and cheese.

Dip the chicken in the flour mixture, shaking off the excess. Dip into the beaten eggs, then evenly coat with the crumb mixture. Arrange the chicken in the prepared pan.

Bake for 40 minutes, or until a thermometer inserted in the thickest portion registers 170°F and the juices run clear.

Makes 4 servings

Per serving: 302 calories, 40 g protein, 21 g carbohydrates, 6 g fat, 192 mg cholesterol, 1 g fiber, 642 mg sodium

Chicken Mirabella

½ cup prunes, halved

¼ cup pimiento-stuffed green olives, halved

⅓ cup chicken broth

⅓ cup red wine vinegar

3 cloves garlic, minced

2 teaspoons dried oregano

½ teaspoon salt

¼ teaspoon freshly ground black pepper

4 bone-in chicken breast halves, skinned

3 tablespoons brown sugar

½ cup dry white wine or vermouth

These marinated chicken breasts bake up moist and tender. The rich sauce is best served over rice, bulgur, or couscous.

In a 13" x 9" baking dish, combine the prunes, olives, broth, vinegar, garlic, oregano, salt, and pepper. Place the chicken, meat side down, in the pan. Cover and refrigerate for at least 4 hours or up to 12 hours, basting occasionally with the marinade.

Preheat the oven to 350°F.

Turn the chicken meat side up. Sprinkle the chicken with the brown sugar and wine and baste with some of the marinade. Bake, basting occasionally, for 45 minutes, or until a thermometer inserted in the thickest portion registers 170°F and the juices run clear.

Makes 4 servings

Per serving: 281 calories, 34 g protein, 26 g carbohydrates, 3 g fat, 82 mg cholesterol, 2 g fiber, 627 mg sodium

Jerk Chicken with Mango

2   **jalapeño chile peppers, halved and seeded (wear plastic gloves when handling)**

1   **shallot, halved**

2   **cloves garlic**

1   **slice (¼" thick) peeled fresh ginger**

2   **tablespoons olive oil**

2   **teaspoons red wine vinegar**

1½   **teaspoons dried thyme**

1   **teaspoon ground allspice**

¼   **teaspoon salt**

4   **bone-in chicken breast halves, skinned**

1   **ripe mango, peeled and chopped**

Fresh mango balances the spicy chicken for a lively dish. Feel free to substitute peaches in place of the mango.

Preheat the oven to 450°F. Coat a 13" x 9" baking pan with cooking spray.

In a food processor, combine the peppers, shallot, garlic, ginger, oil, vinegar, thyme, allspice, and salt. Process, scraping the sides of the container occasionally, until very finely chopped.

Spread the jalapeño mixture on both sides of the chicken breasts. Place the chicken, meat side up, in the prepared baking pan. Bake for 40 minutes, or until a thermometer inserted in the thickest portion registers 170°F and the juices run clear. To serve, sprinkle the mango over the chicken.

Makes 4 servings

Per serving: 246 calories, 30 g protein, 11 g carbohydrates, 9 g fat, 74 mg cholesterol, 1 g fiber, 231 mg sodium

Roasted Chicken with White Beans

4   **boneless, skinless chicken breast halves**

    Salt

    Freshly ground black pepper

1   **can (14–19 ounces) cannellini beans, rinsed and drained**

2   **lemons**

¼   **cup olive or vegetable oil**

3   **cloves garlic, crushed**

1   **tablespoon fresh minced tarragon or 1 teaspoon dried tarragon, crushed**

Fresh lemon and tarragon bring out the natural rich flavors of chicken and beans. A metal pan will brown the dish more than a glass baking dish.

Preheat the oven to 375°F. Coat an 11" x 7" roasting pan with cooking spray.

Arrange the chicken in the prepared pan and season with salt and pepper to taste. Arrange the beans around the chicken.

Cut one of the lemons into wedges and set aside. Into a small bowl, grate ½ teaspoon of peel from the second lemon and squeeze 3 tablespoons juice. Add the oil, garlic, and tarragon and whisk until blended. Drizzle over the chicken and beans. Scatter the lemon wedges over the chicken and beans.

Bake for 30 minutes, or until a thermometer inserted in the thickest portion registers 160°F and the juices run clear.

Makes 4 servings

Per serving: 412 calories, 37 g protein, 35 g carbohydrates, 16 g fat, 66 mg cholesterol, 10 g fiber, 668 mg sodium

Potpie with Thyme Biscuits

1   **pound boneless, skinless chicken breasts, cut into 1" pieces**

½   **teaspoon salt**

¼   **teaspoon freshly ground black pepper**

1   **tablespoon olive or vegetable oil**

2   **cups assorted frozen vegetables such as carrots, pearl onions, and/or sugar snap peas, thawed and drained**

1   **can (14¾ ounces) cream-style corn**

¾   **cup milk**

1   **cup biscuit mix**

½   **teaspoon dried thyme**

Classic potpie can take hours to prepare. This recipe uses frozen vegetables and cream-style corn to create a tasty dish with minimal work.

Preheat the oven to 400°F.

Season the chicken with the salt and pepper. Heat the oil in a medium skillet over medium-high heat. Add the chicken and cook, stirring occasionally, for 8 minutes, or until browned.

In a 3-quart baking dish, combine the chicken, thawed vegetables, corn, and ¼ cup of the milk. Cover and bake for 25 minutes.

Meanwhile, in a small bowl, combine the biscuit mix and thyme. Stir in the remaining ½ cup milk to form a soft dough.

Remove the baking dish from the oven and uncover. Drop the dough by tablespoons over the chicken and vegetables. Bake for 10 minutes, or until the biscuits are golden.

Makes 4 servings

Per serving: 441 calories, 35 g protein, 52 g carbohydrates, 11 g fat, 72 mg cholesterol, 6 g fiber, 1,081 mg sodium

Parmesan Chicken Schnitzel

¼ **cup seasoned dry bread crumbs**

¼ **cup grated Parmesan cheese**

½ **teaspoon freshly ground black pepper**

¼ **teaspoon salt**

1 **egg**

1 **pound thinly sliced boneless, skinless chicken breasts**

2 **tablespoons melted butter**

These versatile cutlets make a great last-minute dinner. Serve with applesauce, salsa, barbecue sauce, or guacamole for dipping.

Preheat the oven to 450°F. Coat a baking sheet with cooking spray.

In a shallow bowl, combine the bread crumbs, cheese, pepper, and salt. In another shallow bowl, beat the egg. Dip the chicken into the egg, letting any excess drip off. Then dip into the bread-crumb mixture, pressing the mixture onto both sides. Place the cutlets in a single layer on the prepared baking sheet. Drizzle with the butter.

Bake for 15 minutes, or until browned and no longer pink and the juices run clear.

Makes 4 servings
Per serving: 253 calories, 31 g protein, 5 g carbohydrates, 11 g fat, 140 mg cholesterol, 1 g fiber, 471 mg sodium

Buttermilk-Battered Chicken

⅔ cup unbleached all-purpose flour

1 teaspoon salt

1 teaspoon dried thyme

½ teaspoon paprika

1 cup buttermilk

2 tablespoons olive or vegetable oil

2 tablespoons Dijon mustard

6 bone-in chicken breast halves, skinned

Serve this southern-inspired chicken with coleslaw and cornbread for a truly regional meal.

Preheat the oven to 400°F. Coat a baking sheet with cooking spray.

In a shallow bowl, combine the flour, salt, thyme, and paprika. Stir in the buttermilk, oil, and mustard until blended.

Dip the chicken into the batter until evenly coated. Place on the prepared baking sheet.

Bake for 40 minutes, or until a thermometer inserted in the thickest portion registers 170°F and the juices run clear.

Makes 4 servings.

Per serving: 332 calories, 38 g protein, 21 g carbohydrates, 10 g fat, 85 mg cholesterol, 1 g fiber, 781 mg sodium

Sweet-and-Spicy Stuffed Chicken

2   **tablespoons olive or vegetable oil**

4   **ounces mushrooms, finely chopped**

1   **scallion, minced**

2   **cups cornbread, herb, or chicken-seasoned stuffing mix**

8   **boneless, skinless chicken breast halves, pounded thin**

1   **egg, beaten**

½   **cup seasoned bread crumbs**

½   **small red bell pepper, finely chopped**

½   **cup apple jelly**

1   **tablespoon Dijon mustard**

¼   **teaspoon hot-pepper sauce**

Spooning a sweet jelly sauce over the chicken just as it finishes baking gives it an extra bit of moisture. Each bite just melts in your mouth.

Preheat the oven to 350°F. Coat a 13" x 9" baking pan with cooking spray.

In a large skillet over medium-high heat, heat 1 tablespoon of the oil. Cook the mushrooms, stirring occasionally, for 4 minutes. Add the scallion and cook for 1 minute. Remove from the heat.

Prepare the stuffing mix according to package directions. Stir the mushroom mixture. Spoon about ½ cup of the mixture onto each chicken breast and pat the stuffing evenly over the chicken. Roll the chicken around the stuffing and secure with a wooden pick. Roll the stuffed chicken in the egg and then in the bread crumbs. Transfer to the prepared baking pan. Bake for 25 minutes, or until the chicken is no longer pink. Do not turn off the oven.

Meanwhile, in the same skillet, heat the remaining 1 tablespoon of oil over medium-high heat and cook the bell pepper, stirring occasionally, for 4 minutes. Stir in the jelly, mustard, and hot-pepper sauce and cook for 2 minutes. Spoon the sauce evenly over the rolls and bake for an additional 5 minutes.

Slice the chicken rolls and serve.

Makes 8 servings

Per serving: 307 calories, 30 g protein, 30 g carbohydrates, 7 g fat, 92 mg cholesterol, 1 g fiber, 563 mg sodium

Baked Pesto Chicken

½ cup seasoned dry bread crumbs

2 tablespoons finely chopped, drained sun-dried tomatoes packed in oil, 1 tablespoon of oil reserved

½ teaspoon cracked black pepper

¼ cup prepared pesto

4 bone-in skinless chicken breast halves

Delicious hot from the oven, this flavor-packed chicken is also wonderful cold. Made ahead and refrigerated for up to three days, this dish is perfect for a picnic.

Preheat the oven to 375°F. Coat a 13" x 9" baking pan with cooking spray.

In a shallow bowl, combine the bread crumbs, tomatoes, and pepper. Spread the pesto on the top side of the chicken breasts, then dip in the bread-crumb mixture, pressing to coat evenly. Arrange the chicken, breast side up, in the prepared pan. Drizzle with the reserved tomato oil.

Bake for 40 minutes, or until a thermometer inserted in the thickest portion registers 170°F and the juices run clear.

Makes 4 servings
Per serving: 267 calories, 33 g protein, 12 g carbohydrates, 9 g fat, 78 mg cholesterol, 1 g fiber, 268 mg sodium

Chicken Fricassee

2   **tablespoons olive or vegetable oil**

1   **chicken (about 3 pounds), skinned and cut up**

1   **large red onion, cut into wedges**

2   **carrots, thinly sliced**

8   **ounces mushrooms, sliced**

2   **cloves garlic, minced**

1   **teaspoon dried rosemary, crushed**

½   **teaspoon freshly ground black pepper**

½   **cup white wine**

2   **cups chicken broth**

1   **large tomato, seeded and chopped**

2   **tablespoons cornstarch**

2   **tablespoons cold water**

A loaf of French bread and a bottle of Sauvignon Blanc will turn this hearty stew into a dinner party. For a more casual meal, serve with a salad and perhaps a glass of milk.

Preheat the oven to 400°F.

Heat the oil in a Dutch oven or large ovenproof saucepan over medium-high heat. Add the chicken and cook for 8 minutes, or until browned on all sides. Remove to a plate and keep warm.

Add the onion, carrots, mushrooms, garlic, rosemary, and pepper to the pot and cook, stirring occasionally, for 8 minutes, or until browned. Add the wine and cook for 2 minutes, stirring to loosen any browned bits.

Add the chicken, broth, and tomato. Bring to a boil over high heat. Cover and bake for 25 minutes, or until a thermometer inserted in the thickest portion of chicken registers 170°F and the juices run clear. Remove the chicken to a serving platter and cover loosely with foil to keep warm.

In a small cup, whisk together the cornstarch and water. Place the Dutch oven over medium-high heat and stir in the cornstarch mixture. Cook for 3 minutes, or until thickened. Return the chicken to the pot and serve.

Makes 4 servings

Per serving: 331 calories, 42 g protein, 13 g carbohydrates, 10 g fat, 99 mg cholesterol, 2 g fiber, 415 mg sodium

California Chicken

1   **tablespoon whole grain mustard**

1   **egg**

1   **cup fresh bread crumbs**

⅓   **cup (1½ ounces) grated Parmesan cheese**

1   **teaspoon grated lemon peel**

4   **boneless, skinless chicken breast halves, pounded to ½" thickness**

1   **bunch watercress, trimmed, or 1 small head leaf lettuce**

3   **large plum tomatoes, chopped**

¼   **cup finely chopped red onion**

¼   **cup chopped fresh basil**

1   **tablespoon balsamic vinegar**

2   **teaspoons extra-virgin olive oil**

⅛   **teaspoon salt**

The lemon peel and fresh herbs add a big flavor bonus to this breaded chicken dish. You can experiment with your own herb combinations for a different twist.

Preheat the oven to 350°F. Coat a broiler pan and rack with cooking spray.

In a shallow bowl, combine the mustard and egg. Beat lightly with a fork. In another shallow bowl, combine the bread crumbs, Parmesan, and lemon peel. Dip the chicken into the mustard mixture, turning to coat, and then into the bread-crumb mixture, pressing the mixture onto both sides. Place the chicken on the rack in the prepared pan.

Cook for 20 minutes, turning once, or until golden brown and a thermometer inserted in the thickest portion registers 160°F and the juices run clear.

Meanwhile, in a medium bowl, combine the watercress or lettuce, tomatoes, onion, basil, vinegar, oil, and salt. Evenly divide the salad among 4 plates. Top each with a chicken breast.

Makes 4 servings
Per serving: 433 calories, 53 g protein, 26 g carbohydrates, 11 g fat, 178 mg cholesterol, 2 g fiber, 641 mg sodium

Honey-Mustard Chicken Dinner

1 **pound boneless, skinless chicken thighs**

1 **large yellow or green bell pepper, cut into 1" pieces**

1 **large red onion, cut into wedges**

3 **tablespoons olive or vegetable oil**

3 **tablespoons honey**

2 **tablespoons balsamic vinegar**

2 **tablespoons Dijon mustard**

4 **garlic cloves, minced**

¼ **teaspoon salt**

1 **cup converted rice**

This colorful dish comes together in minutes, so you can relax while it cooks. Served over rice, it is a meal in itself.

Preheat the oven to 425°F.

Place the chicken, pepper, and onion in a 13" x 9" baking dish. In a small bowl, whisk together the oil, honey, vinegar, mustard, garlic, and salt. Drizzle over the chicken and vegetables. Toss to coat well.

Bake for 40 minutes, or until the chicken is cooked through and is no longer pink and the vegetables are tender.

Meanwhile, 20 minutes before the chicken is finished, prepare the rice according to package directions. Serve with the chicken.

Makes 4 servings

Per serving: 475 calories, 27 g protein, 56 g carbohydrates, 16 g fat, 94 mg cholesterol, 2 g fiber, 290 mg sodium

Tex-Mex Arroz con Pollo

1   **tablespoon olive or vegetable oil**

1   **pound boneless, skinless chicken thighs, cut into 2" chunks**

1   **large red bell pepper, chopped**

1   **onion, chopped**

2   **ribs celery, sliced**

2   **teaspoons chili powder**

2   **teaspoons ground cumin**

1   **teaspoon dried oregano**

¾   **cup rice**

1½ **cups chicken broth**

1   **can (14–19 ounces) black beans, rinsed and drained**

1   **tomato, seeded and chopped**

1   **can (4 ounces) chopped green chile peppers**

This hearty stew will become a regular in most homes. The rich flavors meld together for a south-of-the-border comfort food.

Preheat the oven to 375°F.

Heat the oil in a Dutch oven or large ovenproof saucepan over medium-high heat. Add the chicken and cook for 8 minutes, or until browned on all sides. Remove to a plate and set aside. Add the bell pepper, onion, celery, chili powder, cumin, and oregano and cook, stirring occasionally, for 3 minutes.

Stir in the rice, broth, beans, tomato, chile peppers, and chicken. Bring to a boil over high heat. Cover the pot tightly and bake for 25 minutes, or until the rice is tender.

Makes 4 servings

Per serving: 396 calories, 31 g protein, 51 g carbohydrates, 9 g fat, 94 mg cholesterol, 9 g fiber, 554 mg sodium

Portobello Pasta Bake

8 ounces small rigatoni pasta

2 tablespoons olive or vegetable oil

1 pound boneless, skinless chicken breasts, cut into 1" pieces

2 large portobello mushroom caps, sliced

1 onion, halved and sliced

2 red bell peppers, cut into strips

2 cans (10 ounces each) condensed cream of mushroom soup

2 cups chicken broth

2 tablespoons fresh chopped sage or 1 teaspoon rubbed sage

⅓ cup (1½ ounces) grated Parmesan cheese

Comfort food of the 1970s is updated in this rich dish. Fresh vegetables and chicken are blended with mushroom soup and sage for a meal that will bring back memories.

Preheat the oven to 375°F. Coat a 13" x 9" baking dish with cooking spray.

Prepare the pasta according to package directions.

Meanwhile, heat 1 tablespoon of the oil in a large skillet over medium-high heat. Add the chicken and cook, turning once, for 8 minutes, or until golden. Remove to a plate and keep warm.

Heat the remaining 1 tablespoon oil in the same skillet. Add the mushrooms, onion, and peppers and cook, stirring occasionally, for 8 minutes, or until soft.

In a large bowl combine the chicken, pasta, mushroom mixture, soup, broth, and sage. Spoon into the prepared baking dish. Sprinkle with the cheese.

Cover loosely with foil and bake for 20 minutes. Remove the foil and bake for 10 minutes longer, or until hot and bubbly.

Makes 6 servings
Per serving: 419 calories, 28 g protein, 41 g carbohydrates, 15 g fat, 49 mg cholesterol, 3 g fiber, 1,008 mg sodium

Enchilada Casserole

1 tablespoon olive or vegetable oil

1 pound ground chicken

1 can (14–19 ounces) red kidney beans, rinsed and drained

1 avocado, pitted and chopped

1 jar (16 ounces) salsa

1½ cups (6 ounces) shredded Monterey Jack cheese

8 corn tortillas (6" diameter)

1 scallion, sliced

Classic Mexican enchiladas cook up wonderfully as a casserole. It's very filling, so be sure to bring your appetite!

Preheat the oven to 375°F. Coat a 12" x 8" baking dish with cooking spray.

Heat the oil in a large skillet over medium-high heat. Add the chicken and cook, stirring occasionally, for 6 minutes, or until no longer pink.

In a large bowl, combine the chicken, beans, avocado, 1½ cups of the salsa, and 1 cup of the cheese.

On a work surface, fill each tortilla with ⅔ cup of the chicken mixture. Roll up and place, seam side down, in the prepared baking dish.

Spoon the remaining ½ cup salsa over the tortillas. Sprinkle with the remaining ½ cup cheese and the scallion. Cover with foil and bake for 15 minutes. Remove the foil and bake for 5 minutes longer, or until heated through.

Makes 6 servings

Per serving: 498 calories, 29 g protein, 34 g carbohydrates, 29 g fat, 29 mg cholesterol, 9 g fiber, 734 mg sodium

Chicken Mac 'n' Cheese

8   **ounces elbow macaroni**

3   **cups broccoli florets**

2   **tablespoons butter**

1   **shallot, minced**

3   **tablespoons all-purpose unbleached flour**

2   **cups milk**

1½ **cups (6 ounces) smoked Cheddar cheese**

2   **cups cooked rotisserie chicken, cut into chunks**

¼   **cup drained sun-dried tomatoes packed in oil, cut into strips**

2   **tablespoons seasoned dry bread crumbs**

Classic macaroni and cheese gets a new twist by using smoked Cheddar cheese. Adding broccoli, sun-dried tomatoes, and chicken pumps up the dish for a heart-healthy meal.

Preheat the oven to 350°F. Coat a 2-quart baking dish with cooking spray.

Prepare the macaroni according to package directions, adding the broccoli during the last 3 minutes of cooking time.

Meanwhile, melt the butter in a medium saucepan over medium-high heat. Add the shallot and cook, stirring occasionally, for 2 minutes. Sprinkle in the flour and cook, stirring constantly, for 2 minutes. Stir in the milk and cook, stirring constantly, for 4 minutes, or until the milk just boils. Reduce the heat to low, stir in the cheese, and simmer for 2 minutes, or until thickened and the cheese melts.

In the prepared baking dish, combine the macaroni, broccoli, cheese sauce, chicken, and tomatoes. Sprinkle with the bread crumbs. Bake for 30 minutes, or until hot and bubbling.

Makes 6 servings
Per serving: 495 calories, 32 g protein, 41 g carbohydrates, 23 g fat, 98 mg cholesterol, 3 g fiber, 419 mg sodium

Mexican Lasagna

1   **pound boneless, skinless chicken breasts, cut into strips**

1   **large onion, halved and cut into thin wedges**

1   **large clove garlic, minced**

2   **cups (16 ounces) fat-free ricotta cheese**

1   **cup (8 ounces) reduced-fat sour cream**

1   **jar (4 ounces) chopped green chile peppers**

½   **cup chopped fresh cilantro (optional)**

2   **teaspoons ground cumin**

⅛   **teaspoon salt**

3   **cups salsa**

8   **corn tortillas (6" diameter), cut in half**

1¼   **cups (5 ounces) shredded low-fat Monterey Jack cheese**

Corn tortillas create a tender layer that's so delicious filled with chicken, cheese, and salsa. So rich, it's a meal in itself except for maybe some sangría.

Preheat the oven to 350°F. Coat a 13" x 9" baking dish with cooking spray.

Coat a large nonstick skillet with cooking spray and place over medium heat. Add the chicken and cook, turning several times, for 5 minutes, or until no longer pink. Remove to a medium bowl. Wipe the skillet with a paper towel. Coat with cooking spray. Place over medium heat. Add the onion and garlic. Cover and cook, stirring occasionally, for 7 to 8 minutes, or until lightly browned. Add to the chicken in the bowl.

In another medium bowl, combine the ricotta, sour cream, chile peppers, cilantro (if using), cumin, and salt.

Spread 1 cup of the salsa across the bottom of the prepared baking dish. Arrange half of the tortillas evenly over the salsa. Spread half of the ricotta mixture over the tortillas. Top with half of the chicken mixture. Top with 1 cup of the remaining salsa and ½ cup of the Monterey Jack. Repeat the layering sequence with the remaining tortillas, ricotta mixture, and chicken mixture. Sprinkle with the remaining 1 cup of the salsa and ¾ cup cheese.

Bake for 30 minutes, or until heated through. Loosely cover with foil if the cheese browns too quickly.

Makes 8 servings

Per serving: 281 calories, 30 g protein, 20 g carbohydrates, 9 g fat, 61 mg cholesterol, 3 g fiber, 601 mg sodium

Chicken and Pasta Bake

8   ounces fusilli pasta

2   tablespoons olive or
     vegetable oil

1   pound boneless, skinless
     chicken breasts, cut into
     1" pieces

2   scallions, cut onto
     1" pieces

8   ounces assorted wild
     mushrooms such as
     shiitake, portobello,
     and/or crimini, sliced

1   jar (7 ounces) roasted
     red peppers, drained and
     chopped

1½   cups prepared Alfredo
     pasta sauce

3   tablespoons seasoned
     dry bread crumbs

3   tablespoons grated
     Parmesan cheese

This cheesy pleaser gets its creamy goodness from Alfredo pasta sauce. It's yummy mixed with chicken and sautéed vegetables, and the swirly fusilli catches every last drop.

Prepare the pasta according to package directions. Preheat the oven to 400°F. Coat a 2-quart baking dish with cooking spray.

Heat 1 tablespoon of the oil in a large skillet over medium-high heat. Add the chicken and cook, stirring occasionally, for 8 minutes, or until no longer pink. Remove to a large bowl and set aside. Heat the remaining 1 tablespoon of the oil and cook the scallions and mushrooms for 6 minutes, or until tender-crisp.

To the large bowl with the chicken, add the fusilli, mushroom mixture, peppers, and pasta sauce. Toss to coat well. Place in the prepared baking dish.

In a small bowl, combine the bread crumbs and cheese. Sprinkle over the casserole. Cover with foil and bake for 30 minutes. Remove the foil and bake for 5 minutes longer, or until hot and bubbling.

Makes 6 servings
Per serving: 511 calories, 29 g protein, 38 g carbohydrates, 26 g fat, 86 mg cholesterol, 2 g fiber, 473 mg sodium

Smothered Chicken and Vegetables

¼ cup + 2 tablespoons flour

1 whole chicken (about 3 pounds), cut into serving pieces and skinned

2 tablespoons olive or vegetable oil

1 large onion, cut into wedges

8 ounces mushrooms, halved

3 cloves garlic, minced

1½ cups chicken broth

1½ cups apple cider or juice

4 carrots, sliced thick

1 medium rutabaga, peeled and cut into 1½" pieces

½ cup wild rice

1 teaspoon ground cinnamon

½ teaspoon freshly grated nutmeg

This homestyle one-pot meal comes complete with a luscious gravy. You'll love it spooned over hot cooked rice or wide egg noodles.

Preheat the oven to 350°F.

Place ¼ cup of the flour in a resealable plastic bag. Add the chicken, seal the bag, and shake to coat the pieces with the flour.

Heat 1 tablespoon of the oil in a Dutch oven or large oven-proof saucepan over medium-high heat. Add the chicken and brown on all sides. Remove and set aside.

Heat remaining 1 tablespoon oil and cook the onion and mushrooms, stirring occasionally, for 10 minutes, or until browned. Add the garlic and sprinkle with the remaining 2 tablespoons flour. Cook, stirring constantly, for 2 minutes. Add the broth and apple cider or juice and scrape the bottom of the pan to loosen any browned bits.

Add the carrots, rutabaga, rice, cinnamon, nutmeg, and browned chicken. Bring to a boil over high heat. Cover and bake for 1 hour, or until a thermometer inserted in the thickest portion of the chicken registers 170°F and the juices run clear.

Makes 4 servings
Per serving: 505 calories, 45 g protein, 44 g carbohydrates, 14 g fat, 119 mg cholesterol, 7 g fiber, 391 mg sodium

Honey-Roasted Chicken

1   **whole chicken (about 3 pounds)**

⅓   **cup honey**

1   **teaspoon ground cardamom**

⅔–1 **cup chicken broth**

Cardamom and honey create a flavorful glaze for tender chicken. This simple mixture would be delicious on a turkey too—just double the amount.

Preheat the oven to 350°F. Coat a 13" x 9" baking dish with cooking spray. Place the chicken, breast side up, in the prepared baking dish. Pour the honey over the chicken. Lift the skin and spread the honey with a spatula to evenly coat the breast. Sprinkle with the cardamom, rubbing it under the skin. Pour ⅔ cup of the broth into the pan.

Roast for 40 minutes. Add up to ⅓ cup more of the broth, if needed, to prevent the glaze in the pan from burning. Roast for 20 minutes, or until a thermometer inserted in the thickest part of the breast registers 180°F.

Remove the chicken and allow to rest for 10 minutes. Pour the pan juices into a serving dish. Skim off and discard any fat.

To serve, cut the chicken into thin slices. Drizzle with the pan juices or serve them separately.

Makes 6 servings

Per serving: 332 calories, 24 g protein, 15 g carbohydrates, 19 g fat, 96 mg cholesterol, 1 g fiber, 153 mg sodium

Hot Chicken Wings
with Blue Cheese Dressing

24 **chicken drummettes, skinned**

4 **tablespoons hot sauce**

5 **teaspoons white wine vinegar**

¼ **teaspoon garlic powder**

⅓ **cup (1½ ounces) crumbled blue cheese**

1 **cup (8 ounces) sour cream**

1 **scallion, chopped**

1 **teaspoon sugar**

2 **large ribs celery, cut into sticks**

A big splash of hot sauce makes these wings bite back! The smooth blue cheese dressing is a cool contrast to the heat. For a milder version, just go easier on the hot sauce.

Preheat the oven to 400°F. Line a baking sheet with foil. Coat with cooking spray.

In a large bowl, combine the chicken, 2 tablespoons of the hot sauce, 1 teaspoon of the vinegar, and the garlic powder. Toss to coat well. Arrange on the prepared baking sheet. Bake for 12 to 15 minutes, or until the juices run clear when pierced.

Meanwhile, in a serving bowl, combine the blue cheese, sour cream, scallion, 3 teaspoons of the remaining vinegar, and sugar. Stir to mix, mashing the cheese with the back of a spoon.

Remove the chicken from the oven. Drizzle with the remaining 2 tablespoons hot sauce and 1 teaspoon vinegar. Toss to mix. Arrange on a serving platter. Drizzle with any sauce left on the foil. Serve with the blue cheese dressing and celery sticks.

Makes 24 servings
Per serving: 147 calories, 22 g protein, 1 g carbohydrates, 6 g fat, 84 mg cholesterol, 1 g fiber, 167 mg sodium

Chicken and Vegetable Frittata with Cheddar

1   tablespoon butter or margarine

8   ounces boneless, skinless chicken breasts, cut into 1" pieces

1   large potato, finely chopped

1   cup chicken broth

2   cups broccoli florets, steamed

4   eggs

¼   cup milk

1   tablespoon Dijon mustard

¼   teaspoon freshly ground black pepper

½   cup (2 ounces) shredded sharp Cheddar cheese

This simple egg dish is delicious studded with fresh vegetables and sharp cheese. Serve with a loaf of whole grain bread for a complete meal.

Preheat the oven to 350°F. Coat a 9" deep-dish pie plate with cooking spray.

Melt the butter in a large skillet over medium-high heat. Add the chicken and potato and cook, stirring occasionally, for 6 minutes, or until browned. Reduce the heat to medium. Add the broth and cook, stirring occasionally, for 10 minutes, or until the chicken is no longer pink, the potato is tender, and almost all the liquid has evaporated. Stir in the broccoli and place in the prepared pie plate.

In a bowl, beat together the eggs, milk, mustard, pepper, and ¼ cup of the cheese. Pour over the chicken and vegetables and sprinkle with the remaining ¼ cup cheese.

Bake for 10 minutes. Reduce the heat to 325°F and bake for 15 minutes longer, or until the frittata is barely set in the center when the dish is jiggled. Let stand for 5 minutes before cutting.

Makes 4 servings
Per serving: 275 calories, 26 g protein, 11 g carbohydrates, 14 g fat, 271 mg cholesterol, 2 g fiber, 404 mg sodium

ON THE
GRILL

Crispy Cajun Chicken

¼ **cup ketchup**

2 **cloves garlic, minced**

2 **tablespoons brown sugar**

1 **tablespoon chili powder**

1 **tablespoon lime juice**

1 **teaspoon ground cumin**

½ **teaspoon mustard powder**

¼ **teaspoon ground red pepper**

8 **chicken drumsticks, skinned**

Brown sugar and Cajun seasonings come together with a sweet smack that'll have you loving every finger-licking bite. For a fun meal in the summer, serve with piping hot corn on the cob.

Coat the unheated grill rack with cooking spray. Preheat the grill.

In a medium bowl, combine the ketchup, garlic, brown sugar, chili powder, lime juice, cumin, mustard powder, and pepper until blended.

Place the chicken on the rack and grill, turning occasionally, for 15 minutes. Brush the chicken with the seasoning and grill for 15 minutes longer, or until a thermometer inserted in the thickest portion registers 170°F and the juices run clear.

Makes 4 servings

Per serving: 354 calories, 47 g protein, 12 g carbohydrates, 12 g fat, 157 mg cholesterol, 1 g fiber, 401 mg sodium

Balsamic Grilled Chicken Breasts

⅓ cup balsamic vinegar

2 tablespoons olive oil

1 shallot, minced

1 tablespoon fresh chopped rosemary

¼ teaspoon salt

4 boneless, skinless chicken breast halves

A marinade featuring balsamic vinegar and fresh rosemary brings a hint of Italy to these grilled breasts. Cut leftover chicken into strips and serve over a bed of mixed greens and crisp veggies for an easy lunch.

In a medium bowl, whisk together the vinegar, oil, shallot, rosemary, and salt. Add the chicken, tossing to coat well. Cover and refrigerate for up to 3 hours.

Coat the unheated grill rack with cooking spray. Preheat the grill.

Place the chicken on the rack and grill, turning occasionally, for 15 minutes, or until a thermometer inserted in the thickest portion registers 160°F and the juices run clear.

Makes 4 servings

Per serving: 215 calories, 26 g protein, 6 g carbohydrates, 8 g fat, 66 mg cholesterol, 1 g fiber, 223 mg sodium

Spicy Barbecued Chicken

⅓   cup chili sauce

2   tablespoons red wine
    vinegar

1   tablespoon Dijon
    mustard

¼   teaspoon freshly ground
    black pepper

¼   teaspoon ground red
    pepper

4   bone-in chicken legs with
    thighs (12 ounces each),
    skinned and cut in half

Chili sauce and red pepper give these legs a tangy kick. If you want an even hotter flavor, use a spicy variety of Dijon mustard.

Coat the unheated grill rack with cooking spray. Preheat the grill.

In a small bowl, combine the chili sauce, vinegar, mustard, black pepper, and red pepper.

Place the chicken on the rack and grill, turning occasionally, for 15 minutes. Brush the chicken with the sauce and grill, basting with the remaining sauce, for 15 minutes longer, or until a thermometer inserted in the thickest portion registers 170°F and the juices run clear.

Makes 4 servings

Per serving: 236 calories, 35 g protein, 7 g carbohydrates, 7 g fat, 136 mg cholesterol, 1 g fiber, 801 mg sodium

Perfect Picnic Grilled Chicken

¼ **cup prepared barbecue sauce**

½ **cup mango or apricot nectar**

½ **teaspoon ground ginger**

4 **boneless, skinless chicken breast halves**

Fruity barbecue sauce laced with the warmth of ginger makes this chicken glow with flavor. Serve it up at your next outdoor get-together.

Coat the unheated grill rack with cooking spray. Preheat the grill.

In a medium bowl, combine the barbecue sauce, fruit nectar, and ginger.

Place the chicken on the rack and grill, turning occasionally and basting with sauce, for 15 minutes, or until a thermometer inserted in the thickest portion registers 160°F and the juices run clear.

Makes 4 servings

Per serving: 162 calories, 27 g protein, 9 g carbohydrates, 2 g fat, 66 mg cholesterol, 1 g fiber, 241 mg sodium

Chicken Tacos
with Charred Salsa

¼ cup orange juice

2 tablespoons olive or
vegetable oil

3 cloves garlic, minced

½ teaspoon ground cumin

4 boneless, skinless
chicken breasts

8 plum tomatoes

2 jalapeño chile peppers
(wear plastic gloves
when handling)

2 small red onions, halved

2 tablespoons lime juice

¼ cup chopped fresh
cilantro

¼ teaspoon salt

12 taco shells

Shredded lettuce

Grilling vegetables until they're charred gives them a wonderful smoky flavor that's perfect for all sorts of Latin American dishes. Here, charred veggies make a delicious showing in a salsa for orange-marinated chicken. The results are sensational!

In a medium bowl, combine the orange juice, oil, garlic, and cumin. Add the chicken, cover, and refrigerate for 15 minutes to 1 hour.

Meanwhile, coat a grill rack with cooking spray. Preheat the grill.

Place the tomatoes, peppers, and onions on the rack and grill, turning occasionally, for 8 minutes, or until charred on all sides. Remove from the heat and let stand until the vegetables are cool enough to handle.

Remove the chicken from the marinade and place on the grill rack. Grill, turning occasionally, for 15 minutes, or until a thermometer inserted in the thickest portion registers 160°F and the juices run clear. Cut the chicken into thin strips and set aside.

Cut each tomato in half crosswise and squeeze to remove the seeds. Coarsely chop the tomatoes and place in a medium bowl. Remove and discard the skins and seeds from the peppers. Finely chop the peppers and add to the bowl with the tomatoes. Cut the onions into quarters and add to the tomato mixture. Stir in the lime juice, cilantro, and salt.

To serve, fill the taco shells with lettuce and top with the chicken and salsa.

Makes 4 servings
Per serving: 465 calories, 33 g protein, 46 g carbohydrates, 18 g fat, 66 mg cholesterol, 8 g fiber, 395 mg sodium

Lime-Grilled Chicken with Blueberry Salsa

Salsa

1 cup blueberries

1 yellow pepper, chopped

1 small red onion, minced

¼ cup blueberry pourable all-fruit

¼ cup loosely packed fresh basil leaves, cut into strips

¼ teaspoon salt

Chicken and Marinade

¼ cup lime juice

2 tablespoons olive or vegetable oil

2 shallots, minced

¼ teaspoon freshly ground black pepper

4 boneless, skinless chicken breast halves

Refrigerating the salsa and marinade for this dish gives the flavors a chance to blend, allowing for the utmost in taste satisfaction. You'll love the unexpected pairing of sweet fruit with savory basil in the salsa.

To make the salsa: In a medium bowl, combine the blueberries, pepper, onion, all-fruit, basil, and salt. Cover and refrigerate for at least 2 hours.

To make the chicken and marinade: In a medium bowl, whisk together the lime juice, oil, shallots, and pepper. Add the chicken, turning to coat. Cover and refrigerate for up to 3 hours.

Coat the unheated grill rack with cooking spray. Preheat the grill.

Place the chicken on the rack and grill for 10 minutes, or until a thermometer inserted in the thickest portion registers 160°F and the juices run clear. Serve with the salsa.

Makes 4 servings

Per serving: 284 calories, 27 g protein, 25 g carbohydrates, 8 g fat, 66 mg cholesterol, 2 g fiber, 224 mg sodium

Easy Chicken and Vegetables in Foil

4   **boneless, skinless chicken breast halves**

2   **green and/or red bell peppers, cut into strips**

1   **pound red potatoes, thinly sliced**

¼   **cup prepared barbecue sauce**

1   **tablespoon orange juice**

¼   **teaspoon salt**

¼   **teaspoon cracked black pepper**

⅛   **teaspoon ground red pepper**

Individual foil packets make this dish a snap to prepare. You can easily make the packets ahead of time—just refrigerate them until you're ready to grill them.

Coat the unheated grill rack with cooking spray. Preheat the grill.

Place each chicken breast in the center of a 12" x 18" piece of foil. Evenly top with the bell peppers and potatoes.

In a small bowl, combine the barbecue sauce, orange juice, salt, black pepper, and red pepper until blended. Evenly drizzle over the chicken and vegetables.

Bring up 2 long sides of each piece of foil and double-fold with a 1"-wide fold. Double-fold each end to form a packet.

Place the packets, seam side up, on the rack and grill for 25 minutes, or until the vegetables are tender and a thermometer inserted in the thickest portion of a breast registers 160°F and the juices run clear.

Makes 4 servings
Per serving: 245 calories, 30 g protein, 26 g carbohydrates, 2 g fat, 66 mg cholesterol, 4 g fiber, 390 mg sodium

Grilled Chicken Teriyaki

¼ cup soy sauce

2 tablespoons honey

2 cloves garlic, minced

2 tablespoons toasted sesame oil

1 tablespoon sesame seeds, toasted

½ teaspoon grated orange peel

4 bone-in skinless chicken breast halves

This teriyaki-style chicken has a very pleasing smoky taste. The longer you marinate the chicken, the more pronounced the flavor. Grill up some fresh bell peppers and onions to serve on the side.

In a large zip-top plastic bag, combine the soy sauce, honey, garlic, oil, sesame seeds, and orange peel. Add the chicken, seal the bag, and turn to coat. Refrigerate for up to 8 hours, turning occasionally.

Coat the unheated grill rack with cooking spray. Preheat the grill.

Place the chicken on the rack and grill, turning occasionally, for 30 minutes, or until a thermometer inserted in the thickest portion registers 170°F and the juices run clear.

Makes 4 servings

Per serving: 241 calories, 28 g protein, 11 g carbohydrates, 9 g fat, 66 mg cholesterol, 1 g fiber, 1103 mg sodium

Blackened Chicken

2 tablespoons olive oil

4 cloves garlic, minced

2 teaspoons chili powder

2 teaspoons ground cumin

2 teaspoons dried thyme

1 teaspoon ground cinnamon

1 teaspoon freshly ground black pepper

4 boneless, skinless chicken breast halves

Blackening is a cooking technique that was popularized in New Orleans and is used frequently in Cajun-style cuisine. This dish comes together quickly because you combine the seasonings for the spice rub in one speedy step.

Coat the unheated grill rack with cooking spray. Preheat the grill.

In a small bowl, combine the oil, garlic, chili powder, cumin, thyme, cinnamon, and pepper.

Rub both sides of the chicken with the spice mixture. Place the chicken on the rack and grill, turning occasionally, for 15 minutes, or until a thermometer inserted in the thickest portion registers 160°F and the juices run clear.

Makes 4 servings
Per serving: 203 calories, 27 g protein, 3 g carbohydrates, 9 g fat, 66 mg cholesterol, 2 g fiber, 91 mg sodium

Chicken Kebabs

3   **tablespoons olive oil**

3   **tablespoons balsamic vinegar**

2   **tablespoons maple syrup**

1   **tablespoon country Dijon mustard**

2   **cloves garlic, minced**

¼   **teaspoon salt**

¼   **teaspoon freshly ground black pepper**

1   **pound boneless, skinless chicken breasts, cut into 1" pieces**

2   **red and/or green bell peppers, cut into 1" pieces**

1   **large onion, cut into 1" pieces**

Kebabs are always great fun—kids especially like them served right on the skewers. The chicken bursts with a sweet and tangy marinade.

In a 13" x 9" baking dish, combine the oil, vinegar, maple syrup, mustard, garlic, salt, and black pepper. Thread the chicken, bell peppers, and onion alternately onto 8 metal skewers. Lay the skewers in the baking pan and baste with the marinade. Cover and refrigerate for up to 3 hours, turning occasionally.

Coat the unheated grill rack with cooking spray. Preheat the grill.

Place the skewers on the rack and grill, turning occasionally, for 14 minutes, or until the chicken is no longer pink and the vegetables are tender.

Makes 4 servings

Per serving: 290 calories, 27 g protein, 17 g carbohydrates, 12 g fat, 66 mg cholesterol, 2 g fiber, 246 mg sodium

Jamaican Chicken Kebabs

1   piece (1") peeled fresh ginger

1   Scotch bonnet chile pepper, seeded (wear plastic gloves when handling)

¼   cup red wine vinegar

3   tablespoons olive or vegetable oil

1   teaspoon dried thyme

½   teaspoon ground allspice

½   teaspoon salt

1   pound boneless, skinless chicken breasts, cubed

If you like a little heat with your chicken, you've come to the right place! Here, a fiery Scotch bonnet chile pepper is pureed in a marinade for fun and easy kebabs. Use two jalapeño chiles instead for a milder version.

In a blender, process the ginger, pepper, vinegar, oil, thyme, allspice, and salt until nearly smooth.

In a large resealable plastic bag, combine the chicken and marinade. Toss until evenly coated. Cover and refrigerate for up to 3 hours.

Coat the unheated grill rack with cooking spray. Preheat the grill.

Thread the chicken onto metal skewers. Place the skewers on the rack and grill, turning occasionally, for 12 minutes, or until the chicken is no longer pink and the juices run clear.

Makes 4 servings

Per serving: 221 calories, 26 g protein, 2 g carbohydrates, 12 g fat, 66 mg cholesterol, 1 g fiber, 366 mg sodium

---

COOKING TIP

If you're using wooden skewers, be sure to soak them in water for 30 minutes before threading the chicken. Skewers that have not been soaked will burn.

Grilled Chicken and Potato Salad over Greens

½ cup olive or vegetable oil

⅓ cup white wine vinegar

1 shallot, minced

2 cloves garlic, minced

2 tablespoons Dijon mustard

2 tablespoons chopped fresh sage

½ teaspoon salt

¼ teaspoon freshly ground black pepper

2 pounds red-skinned potatoes, cut into ¾" chunks

1 pound boneless, skinless chicken thighs

6 cups salad greens

In this main-dish salad, potatoes and chicken soak up a delicious marinade that does double duty as a dressing for crisp salad greens. This is a truly satisfying salad.

In a medium bowl, whisk together the oil, vinegar, shallot, garlic, mustard, sage, salt, and pepper. Reserve 3 tablespoons of the marinade.

In a large bowl, combine the potatoes and half of the marinade and toss until evenly coated. Add the chicken to the bowl with the remaining marinade, turning the chicken until evenly coated.

Coat the unheated grill rack with cooking spray. Preheat grill.

Tear two 18" x 24" pieces of foil and stack to make a double layer. Spoon the potato mixture in the center and fold the foil in half so that the seams are along the edges. Seal the edges tightly with double folds. Place the packet on the rack and grill, turning and shaking occasionally, for 30 minutes, or until the potatoes are tender.

Remove the chicken from the marinade and grill, turning occasionally, for 15 minutes, or until a thermometer inserted in the thickest portion registers 160°F and the juices run clear. Cut the chicken into strips.

Place the greens in a serving bowl and toss with the reserved marinade. Top with the potatoes and chicken.

Makes 4 servings

Per serving: 576 calories, 30 g protein, 40 g carbohydrates, 33 g fat, 94 mg cholesterol, 6 g fiber, 454 mg sodium

Chicken Rosemary Fingers

¼ **cup lemon juice**

3 **tablespoons olive oil**

1 **clove garlic, minced**

2 **tablespoons chopped fresh rosemary**

¼ **teaspoon salt**

¼ **teaspoon freshly ground black pepper**

1 **pound boneless, skinless chicken breast halves, cut into thick strips**

Lemon and rosemary blend divinely in these savory strips of chicken. Serve them with a crunchy salad for a light lunch, or as the star appetizer at your next party.

In a medium bowl, whisk together the lemon juice, oil, garlic, rosemary, salt, and pepper. Add the chicken and toss until evenly coated. Cover and refrigerate for up to 3 hours.

Coat the unheated grill rack with cooking spray. Preheat the grill.

Place the chicken on the rack and grill, turning occasionally, for 6 minutes, or until the chicken is no longer pink and the juices run clear.

Makes 4 servings

Per serving: 221 calories, 26 g protein, 2 g carbohydrates, 12 g fat, 66 mg cholesterol, 1 g fiber, 220 mg sodium

COOKING TIP

Serve these chicken fingers with a heavenly mustard dipping sauce you can make yourself. Just combine 2 tablespoons prepared honey-mustard with 2 tablespoons mayonnaise—it's that easy!

Grilled Chicken Burgers with Vegetable Salsa

Chicken Burgers

1¼ pounds ground chicken

½ cup (2 ounces) shredded mozzarella or Monterey Jack cheese

2 cloves garlic, minced

½ teaspoon salt

¼ teaspoon freshly ground black pepper

Salsa

1 tablespoon olive oil

1 tablespoon balsamic vinegar

¼ teaspoon salt

½ tomato, seeded and chopped

½ small cucumber, peeled, seeded, and chopped

½ small red onion, finely chopped

½ yellow bell pepper, chopped

These burgers are terrific for lunch or a casual supper. If you like, you can lightly toast hamburger buns on the upper grill rack, then top the burgers with crispy greens and the vegetable salsa.

To make the chicken burgers: In a medium bowl, combine the chicken, cheese, garlic, salt, and pepper just until blended. Shape into 4 patties.

To make the salsa: In a large bowl, whisk together the oil, vinegar, and salt. Add the tomato, cucumber, onion, and pepper and toss to coat well. Set aside.

Coat the unheated grill rack with cooking spray. Preheat the grill.

Place the burgers on the rack and grill for 20 minutes, or until a thermometer inserted in the center registers 165°F and the meat is no longer pink.

Serve the burgers with salsa.

Makes 4 servings
Per serving: 303 calories, 37 g protein, 11 g carbohydrates, 12 g fat, 93 mg cholesterol, 2 g fiber, 588 mg sodium

---

COOKING TIP

You'll notice that ground chicken tends to get mushier the more you work with it. It's best to form and shape the patties quickly, handling the ground chicken as little as possible.

AT THE
READY

Chinese Chicken Salad

8   **wonton wrappers, cut into ¼"-wide strips**

¼   **cup rice wine or white wine vinegar**

2   **tablespoons hoisin sauce**

2   **tablespoons olive or vegetable oil**

1   **tablespoon grated fresh ginger**

1   **clove garlic, minced**

¼   **teaspoon crushed red-pepper flakes**

8   **cups mixed greens (about 6 ounces)**

2   **cups shredded cooked chicken**

2   **carrots, shredded**

2   **scallions, thinly sliced**

1   **red bell pepper, cut into thin strips**

Crispy wonton strips top this tangy Asian-style salad. If you prefer a milder flavor, you can reduce the amount of red-pepper flakes.

Preheat the oven to 400°F. Coat a baking sheet with cooking spray. Separate the wonton strips and place on the prepared sheet. Coat lightly with cooking spray. Bake for 3 to 5 minutes, or until golden brown and crisp. Remove and set aside.

In a large bowl, whisk together the vinegar, hoisin sauce, oil, ginger, garlic, and red-pepper flakes until blended. Add the greens, chicken, carrots, scallions, bell pepper, and reserved wonton strips. Toss to coat well.

Makes 4 servings
Per serving: 322 calories, 22 g protein, 26 g carbohydrates, 13 g fat, 52 mg cholesterol, 3 g fiber, 299 mg sodium

Mandarin Chicken Toss

8   **wonton wrappers, cut into ¼"-wide strips**

1   **can (11 ounces) mandarin oranges, drained, reserving ⅓ cup syrup**

¼   **cup rice wine or white wine vinegar**

3   **tablespoons toasted sesame oil**

2   **tablespoons soy sauce**

1   **teaspoon grated fresh ginger or ¼ teaspoon ground**

3   **cups cut-up cooked chicken**

1   **red bell pepper, cut into thin strips**

8   **cups shredded romaine lettuce**

¼   **cup loosely packed fresh cilantro leaves**

2   **tablespoons sesame seeds, toasted**

This refreshing salad boasts crunchy, flavorful romaine and juicy strips of chicken dotted with sesame seeds. Mandarin oranges add a burst of contrasting sweetness that will make this dish a favorite.

Preheat the oven to 400°F. Coat a baking sheet with cooking spray. Separate the wonton strips and place on the prepared sheet. Coat lightly with cooking spray. Bake for 3 to 5 minutes, or until golden brown and crisp. Remove and set aside.

In a large bowl, whisk together the reserved mandarin syrup, vinegar, oil, soy sauce, and ginger until blended. Add the chicken, pepper, and oranges. Toss to coat well.

Evenly divide the lettuce among 4 plates. Top with chicken mixture and sprinkle with the wonton strips, cilantro, and sesame seeds.

Makes 4 servings

Per serving: 403 calories, 30 g protein, 24 g carbohydrates, 19 g fat, 77 mg cholesterol, 4 g fiber, 692 mg sodium

Chicken and Corn Salad

3 tablespoons olive oil

3 tablespoons red wine vinegar

1 teaspoon ground cumin

¼ teaspoon salt

2 cups cubed cooked chicken

2 cans (15–17 ounces each) whole kernel corn, drained

1 can (15–19 ounces) black beans, rinsed and drained

1 red bell pepper, chopped

2 scallions, sliced

2 tablespoons chopped fresh cilantro

Bright bell peppers and juicy, sweet corn mingle with wholesome black beans and crunchy scallions to create a delicious splash of color, texture, and taste.

In a large bowl, whisk together the oil, vinegar, cumin, and salt. Add the chicken, corn, beans, pepper, scallions, and cilantro. Toss to coat well.

Makes 4 servings

Per serving: 355 calories, 24 g protein, 38 g carbohydrates, 15 g fat, 50 mg cholesterol, 9 g fiber, 421 mg sodium

New Classics Chicken Salad

¼ cup (2 ounces) plain yogurt

3 tablespoons mayonnaise

2 tablespoons chopped fresh dill

2 tablespoons lemon juice

½ teaspoon salt

⅛ teaspoon freshly ground black pepper

2 cups cut-up cooked chicken

1 can (15½ ounces) chickpeas, rinsed and drained

1 large red bell pepper, finely chopped

1 small cucumber, peeled, seeded, and chopped

1 scallion, sliced

You'll enjoy the down-home fresh flavor of this satisfying chicken salad. Mixing plain yogurt with just a bit of mayo gives it the creaminess you crave with just a fraction of the fat.

In a large bowl, combine the yogurt, mayonnaise, dill, lemon juice, salt, and black pepper. Add the chicken, chickpeas, bell pepper, cucumber, and scallion. Toss to coat well.

Makes 4 servings

Per serving: 343 calories, 23 g protein, 32 g carbohydrates, 15 g fat, 58 mg cholesterol, 7 g fiber, 573 mg sodium

Chicken Tabbouleh

1   **box (5¼ ounces) tabbouleh wheat salad mix**

1   **cup boiling water**

3   **tablespoons olive oil**

¼   **cup orange juice**

2   **tablespoons red wine vinegar**

1   **tablespoon honey**

2   **cups cut-up cooked chicken**

¼   **cup dried apricots, cut into thin strips**

1   **orange bell pepper, finely chopped**

½   **pint pear cherry tomatoes, halved**

Traditional Middle Eastern tabbouleh is made from bulgur wheat. This version uses a convenient wheat salad mix that includes a flavorful spice pack. The unusual addition of apricots creates a nice sweetness. If you like, serve over a bed of mixed greens.

In a large bowl, combine all contents of the tabbouleh wheat salad mix and spice pack, water, and 2 tablespoons of the oil. Cover and let stand for 30 minutes.

Meanwhile, in a small bowl, whisk together the remaining 1 tablespoon oil, orange juice, vinegar, and honey.

Add the chicken, apricots, pepper, tomatoes, and dressing to the tabbouleh and toss to coat well. Serve over salad greens, if desired.

Makes 4 servings

Per serving: 364 calories, 21 g protein, 43 g carbohydrates, 15 g fat, 50 mg cholesterol, 8 g fiber, 397 mg sodium

COOKING TIP

It's easy to cut dried apricots into strips using kitchen shears. The trick is to first coat the shears with cooking spray so that the fruit won't stick.

Chicken Cutlet Sandwiches with Jalapeño Mayo

¼ cup light mayonnaise

¼ cup chopped fresh cilantro

1 small chipotle chile pepper in adobo sauce, minced

1 tablespoon lime juice

⅛ teaspoon freshly ground black pepper

4 whole grain round rolls

4 cooked chicken cutlets

1 medium tomato, cut into 8 thin slices

4 leaves romaine lettuce

½ red onion, thinly sliced

When cooking chicken cutlets for another meal, such as Parmesan Chicken Schnitzel on page 51, cook up some extra ones. When cooled, wrap in plastic wrap. You'll be ready to put together this meal in moments.

In a small bowl, combine the mayonnaise, cilantro, chile pepper, lime juice, and black pepper.

Split the rolls and evenly spread with the mayonnaise mixture. Evenly layer the chicken cutlets, tomato, lettuce, and onion on each sandwich, then top with the other half of the rolls.

Makes 4 servings
Per serving: 322 calories, 31 g protein, 32 g carbohydrates, 9 g fat, 79 mg cholesterol, 3 g fiber, 320 mg sodium

Chicken, Mushroom, and Barley Salad

1   cup quick-cooking barley
¼   cup olive oil
3   tablespoons balsamic vinegar
1   tablespoon Dijon mustard
¼   teaspoon salt
¼   teaspoon freshly ground black pepper
2   cups shredded cooked chicken
4   large mushrooms, thinly sliced
2   scallions, sliced
1   jar (7¼ ounces) roasted red peppers, rinsed, drained, and coarsely chopped
¼   cup packed fresh basil leaves, cut into strips

Barley, a hardy centuries-old grain, takes on a smoky goodness when tossed with roasted red peppers and earthy mushrooms. The Dijon mustard adds a slightly sharp bite.

Prepare the barley according to package directions. Rinse with cold water and drain.

Meanwhile, in a large bowl, whisk together the oil, vinegar, mustard, salt, and black pepper. Add the chicken, mushrooms, scallions, roasted peppers, basil, and cooked barley. Toss to coat well.

Makes 6 servings
Per serving: 264 calories, 14 g protein, 24 g carbohydrates, 13 g fat, 34 mg cholesterol, 4 g fiber, 149 mg sodium

Autumn Chicken Salad

½ cup (4 ounces) sour cream

¼ cup light mayonnaise

1 tablespoon chopped fresh thyme or 1 teaspoon dried

1 tablespoon lemon juice

½ teaspoon grated lemon peel

½ teaspoon salt

4 cups cubed cooked chicken

2 ribs celery, chopped

1 red pear, cut into ½" cubes

1 head Boston or bibb lettuce

¼ cup finely chopped pecans, toasted

You'll love the sweetness of a juicy red pear atop bright and crisp lettuce. Chopped walnuts lend a savory flair and extra crunch.

In a large bowl, combine the sour cream, mayonnaise, thyme, lemon juice, lemon peel, and salt. Add the chicken, celery, and pear. Toss to coat well. Cover and refrigerate for at least 1 hour.

Evenly divide the lettuce among 4 plates. Top with the chicken salad and sprinkle with the pecans.

Makes 4 servings

Per serving: 450 calories, 37 g protein, 15 g carbohydrates, 27 g fat, 118 mg cholesterol, 2 g fiber, 514 mg sodium

Asian Chicken Roll-Ups

1   **can (11 ounces) mandarin oranges, drained, reserving 2 tablespoons syrup**

¼   **cup plum sauce**

1   **tablespoon rice wine or wine vinegar**

1   **tablespoon grated fresh ginger**

4   **cups cooked chicken cut into thin strips**

1   **red bell pepper, chopped**

½   **small English cucumber, peeled, seeded, and chopped**

2   **scallions, thinly sliced on the diagonal**

4   **whole wheat tortillas (8" diameter)**

8   **leaves romaine lettuce**

Luscious plum sauce and mandarin oranges give these roll-ups their distinctive Asian flavor. They make a terrific take-along lunch.

In a large bowl, whisk together the reserved mandarin syrup, plum sauce, vinegar, and ginger. Add the oranges, chicken, pepper, cucumber, and scallions and toss to coat well.

Wrap the tortillas in paper towels and microwave on high for 30 seconds, or until warmed. Place on a work surface. Place 2 lettuce leaves on each tortilla. Evenly divide the salad on the lettuce. Roll into cylinders and slice in half diagonally.

Makes 4 servings
Per serving: 348 calories, 36 g protein, 29 g carbohydrates, 9 g fat, 101 mg cholesterol, 10 g fiber, 286 mg sodium

Cobb Salad
with Parmesan Dressing

½ cup buttermilk

2 tablespoons grated
   Parmesan cheese

¼ cup (2 ounces) reduced-
   fat sour cream

1 tablespoon balsamic
   vinegar

¼ cup packed fresh basil
   leaves, cut into thin
   strips

½ teaspoon coarsely
   cracked black pepper

2 cups mixed salad
   greens, such as romaine
   or chicory

3 cups smoked chicken
   cut into strips

⅓ cup (1½ ounces) low-fat
   feta cheese

2 red and/or yellow bell
   peppers, chopped

1 small red onion, chopped

4 hard-cooked egg whites,
   finely chopped

4 slices turkey bacon,
   cooked, drained, and
   crumbled

Cobb salad, made famous at Hollywood's Brown Derby restaurant, makes a lovely presentation. It's both sweet and smoky, satisfying all your taste buds.

To make the dressing, in a small bowl, combine the buttermilk, Parmesan, sour cream, vinegar, basil, and pepper.

Divide the greens among 4 salad plates. Top with the chicken, mounding it in the center of the greens. Evenly mound the feta on the greens. Arrange small mounds of peppers, onion, and egg whites over the greens. Sprinkle with the turkey bacon. Serve with the Parmesan dressing.

Makes 4 servings
Per serving: 289 calories, 32 g protein, 8 g carbohydrates, 14 g fat, 103 mg cholesterol, 2 g fiber, 469 mg sodium

Quick Chicken Wraps

¼ cup tahini (sesame paste)

2 tablespoons sesame oil

2 tablespoons soy sauce

2 tablespoons lime juice

2 cups cooked chicken cut into thin strips

4 cups shredded green cabbage

2 carrots, shredded

1 red bell pepper, cut into thin strips

8 flour tortillas (6" diameter)

What a dazzling combination! Chicken is joined by plenty of vegetables as well as a splash of nutty sesame and just a hint of lime.

In a large bowl, whisk together the tahini, oil, soy sauce, and lime juice. Add the chicken, cabbage, carrots, and pepper. Toss to coat well.

Wrap the tortillas in paper towels and microwave on high for 30 seconds, or until warmed. Evenly divide the chicken mixture down the center of each tortilla. Fold the bottom end in toward the center, then fold in the sides.

Makes 4 servings

Per serving: 506 calories, 26 g protein, 49 g carbohydrates, 23 g fat, 50 mg cholesterol, 7 g fiber, 909 mg sodium

Chicken Pesto Pizza

1   12" prebaked pizza shell
⅓   cup prepared pesto
1   cup cooked chicken cut into small strips
1   roasted red pepper, cut into small strips
½   cup water-packed canned artichoke hearts, rinsed and drained, patted dry and quartered
½   cup (2 ounces) crumbled goat cheese

A prebaked pizza shell is the secret to this quick and easy dish—great for those rushed weeknights! Or serve as an appetizer the next time you have company.

Preheat the oven to 450°F. Place the pizza shell on a baking sheet.

Evenly spread the pesto over the crust. Arrange the chicken, pepper strips, and artichokes over the pesto. Top with the cheese.

Bake for 10 minutes, or until heated through and the crust is crisp.

Makes 4 servings

Per serving: 485 calories, 30 g protein, 55 g carbohydrates, 17 g fat, 56 mg cholesterol, 3 g fiber, 823 mg sodium

Barbecue Chicken and Cheddar Calzones

1   tablespoon cornmeal

1   large onion, halved and thinly sliced

2   cups cooked and shredded chicken

1   cup barbecue sauce

2   tubes (10 ounces each) refrigerated pizza dough

1   cup (4 ounces) shredded low-fat Cheddar cheese

1   egg, lightly beaten with 1 teaspoon water

These calzones are really quite easy to put together, and they're great as an on-the-go lunch. You can experiment with the flavor by trying different varieties of barbecue sauce.

Preheat the oven to 375°F. Coat a baking sheet with cooking spray. Sprinkle with the cornmeal.

Coat a medium nonstick skillet with cooking spray and set over medium heat. Add the onion and cook, stirring occasionally, for 5 minutes, or until soft. Add the chicken and barbecue sauce and toss to coat.

Turn the dough out onto a lightly floured work surface. Divide the dough into 4 equal pieces. Roll 1 piece of dough into a 7" circle. Place ¼ of the chicken mixture on 1 side of the circle, spreading to within 1" of the edge. Sprinkle with ¼ cup of the cheese. Brush the edges of the crust with some of the egg mixture. Fold the circle in half. Pinch the edges to seal. Repeat with the remaining dough and filling to make a total of 4 calzones.

Place on the prepared baking sheet. Brush the calzones with the remaining egg mixture. With a sharp knife, make 3 small slashes in the top of each calzone.

Bake for 20 minutes, or until the crusts are golden brown. To serve, cut each calzone in half.

Makes 8 servings

Per serving: 357 calories, 24 g protein, 51 g carbohydrates, 5 g fat, 39 mg cholesterol, 3 g fiber, 673 mg sodium

Open-Faced Chicken Quesadilla

4   **flour tortillas (10" diameter)**

½   **cup mayonnaise**

1   **tablespoon roasted garlic and red pepper spice blend**

2   **cups shredded cooked chicken**

1   **cup (4 ounces) shredded Monterey Jack cheese**

2   **medium tomatoes, seeded and chopped**

2   **cups shredded romaine lettuce**

This is the easiest quesadilla ever—you don't have to flip it in the pan! Serve with sour cream and guacamole on the side.

Preheat the oven to 350°F. Place the tortillas on baking sheets and toast for 5 minutes.

In a small bowl, combine the mayonnaise and the spice blend. Spread 2 tablespoons of the mixture over each tortilla. Evenly top the center of each tortilla with chicken, then sprinkle with cheese. Arrange the tomatoes around the chicken. Bake for 10 minutes, or until heated through. Sprinkle the lettuce around the tomato.

Makes 4 servings

Per serving: 434 calories, 27 g protein, 26 g carbohydrates, 25 g fat, 85 mg cholesterol, 2 g fiber, 540 mg sodium

Southern Barbecue Pizza

1   teaspoon cornmeal

1   tube (10 ounces) refrigerated pizza dough

1   tablespoon olive or vegetable oil

1   red bell pepper, cut into strips

1   red onion, thinly sliced

2   cups shredded cooked chicken

½   cup barbecue sauce

½   cup (2 ounces) shredded Monterey Jack cheese

½   cup (2 ounces) shredded sharp Cheddar cheese

Try this sizzling southern take on a national favorite. Barbecue sauce and sharp cheeses give it the extra snap. If you're in a hurry, you can use a prebaked pizza shell instead of the pizza dough.

Preheat the oven to 425°F. Coat a baking sheet with cooking spray. Sprinkle with the cornmeal.

Shape the pizza crust into a 10" circle. Place on the prepared baking sheet.

Heat the oil in a large skillet over medium-high heat. Add the pepper and onion and cook, stirring occasionally, for 5 minutes, or until tender-crisp.

In a medium bowl, combine the chicken and ¼ cup of the barbecue sauce.

Spread the remaining ¼ cup barbecue sauce over the dough. Top with the chicken and vegetables. Sprinkle with the cheeses.

Bake for 15 minutes, or until the bottom of the crust is browned and the cheese is melted.

Makes 4 servings
Per serving: 455 calories, 29 g protein, 43 g carbohydrates, 19 g fat, 78 mg cholesterol, 3 g fiber, 663 mg sodium

Pitas with Chicken-in-the-Slaw

¼   cup (2 ounces) lemon
     yogurt

3   tablespoons mayonnaise

1½ cups cubed cooked
     chicken

1   cup shredded red and/or
     green cabbage

2   carrots, shredded

1   red or green apple, cored
     and chopped

⅓   cup raisins

¼   teaspoon cracked black
     pepper

4   pitas (8" diameter)

Here's a great make-ahead sandwich filling—the cabbage stays crunchy hours after the filling has been made.

In a medium bowl, combine the yogurt and mayonnaise. Add the chicken, cabbage, carrots, apple, raisins, and pepper and toss to coat well.

Cut one ½"-wide strip off the edge of each pita, forming a pocket. Evenly divide the chicken mixture among the pitas.

Makes 4 servings

Per serving: 426 calories, 22 g protein, 55 g carbohydrates, 13 g fat, 54 mg cholesterol, 4 g fiber, 451 mg sodium

Index

Boldface references indicate photographs.

CONVERSION CHART

These equivalents have been slightly rounded to make measuring easier.

VOLUME MEASUREMENTS

U.S.	Imperial	Metric
¼ tsp	–	1 ml
½ tsp	–	2 ml
1 tsp	–	5 ml
1 Tbsp	–	15 ml
2 Tbsp (1 oz)	1 fl oz	30 ml
¼ cup (2 oz)	2 fl oz	60 ml
⅓ cup (3 oz)	3 fl oz	80 ml
½ cup (4 oz)	4 fl oz	120 ml
⅔ cup (5 oz)	5 fl oz	160 ml
¾ cup (6 oz)	6 fl oz	180 ml
1 cup (8 oz)	8 fl oz	240 ml

WEIGHT MEASUREMENTS

U.S.	Metric
1 oz	30 g
2 oz	60 g
4 oz (¼ lb)	115 g
5 oz (⅓ lb)	145 g
6 oz	170 g
7 oz	200 g
8 oz (½ lb)	230 g
10 oz	285 g
12 oz (¾ lb)	340 g
14 oz	400 g
16 oz (1 lb)	455 g
2.2 lb	1 kg

LENGTH MEASUREMENTS

U.S.	Metric
¼"	0.6 cm
½"	1.25 cm
1"	2.5 cm
2"	5 cm
4"	11 cm
6"	15 cm
8"	20 cm
10"	25 cm
12" (1')	30 cm

PAN SIZES

U.S.	Metric
8" cake pan	20 × 4 cm sandwich or cake tin
9" cake pan	23 × 3.5 cm sandwich or cake tin
11" × 7" baking pan	28 × 18 cm baking tin
13" × 9" baking pan	32.5 × 23 cm baking tin
15" × 10" baking pan	38 × 25.5 cm baking tin (Swiss roll tin)
2 qt rectangular baking dish	30 × 19 cm baking dish
1½ qt baking dish	1.5 liter baking dish
2 qt baking dish	2 liter baking dish
9" pie plate	22 × 4 or 23 × 4 cm pie plate
7" or 8" springform pan	18 or 20 cm springform or loose-bottom cake tin
9" × 5" loaf pan	23 × 13 cm or 2 lb narrow loaf tin or pâté tin

TEMPERATURES

Fahrenheit	Centigrade	Gas
140°	60°	–
160°	70°	–
180°	80°	–
225°	110°	–
250°	120°	½
300°	150°	2
325°	160°	3
350°	180°	4
375°	190°	5
400°	200°	6
450°	230°	8
500°	260°	–